TALES OF A HOLLYWOOD HOUSEWIFE

TALES OF A HOLLYWOOD HOUSEWIFE

A Memoir by The First Mrs. Lee Marvin

BETTY MARVIN

iUniverse, Inc.
Bloomington

TALES OF A HOLLYWOOD HOUSEWIFE
A MEMOIR BY THE FIRST MRS. LEE MARVIN

iUniverse books may be ordered through booksellers or by contacting:

iUniverse
1663 Liberty Drive
Bloomington, IN 47403
www.iuniverse.com
1-800-Authors (1-800-288-4677)

ISBN: 978-1-4620-4688-1 (sc)
ISBN: 978-1-4620-4700-0 (ebk)

Printed in the United States of America

iUniverse rev. date: 08/25/2011

With love to my four children, Christopher, Courtenay, Cynthia, and Claudia.

And thanks to their father, Lee, for the adventure.

CHAPTER TITLES

ENDORSEMENT

This is not just another "Hollywood story." Betty's marriage to Lee Marvin will take you on a sweeping journey, from rags to riches and back to rags. To be able to emerge as a survivor from those tumultuous Hollywood days is remarkable. It takes guts to keep marching forward. Betty does just that in her entertaining, humorous, and poignant memoir.

—Tab Hunter

ACKNOWLEDGMENTS

To my poet friend Shirley Windward, for encouraging me to write and showing me how; Kathryn Harrison, for her support; and Gila Sand, for her invaluable assistance.

PREFACE

Except for seeing very few movies when I was growing up in the small river town of Sedro-Woolley, Washington and imitating the Judy Garland songs and dances seen in those movies, I had no knowledge of or interest in Hollywood. I was taught to play the piano and given an appreciation of all the arts by my Grandma Ebeling, In 1945, after graduating from high school at sixteen, I ran away to find my father in Los Angeles, with the dream of majoring in music at UCLA.

Daddy turned out to be a bigger-than-life character who was partially responsible for introducing me to an exciting adventure. Getting to know him was an education in itself. I made great friends in the music and theatre departments at college, and loved my classes, particularly my voice lessons with Erv Windward. But it was pure serendipity that I should be taken by my roommate Joanne to her cousin Lauren Bacall's home to have Christmas dinner with them and her husband Humphrey Bogart. It was also a stroke of fate that my school friend and singing partner, Jerry, should introduce me to Roger Edens, head music producer at MGM, who began coaching me for a musical comedy career. After leaving UCLA in 1949, I got even closer to the Hollywood life by becoming the nanny to Joan Crawford's four children. This turned out to be a bittersweet experience which lasted two years. I was still very intent on having a career either in opera or in musical comedy and put all my spare time and money into this pursuit.

I was certainly not prepared at twenty-four for a whirlwind courtship and marriage to Lee Marvin, who was just getting started as an actor in Hollywood. I put aside seven years of voice training because my husband declared there would be only one career in the family. I had been taught as a young girl that marriage and family were the only important goals in life, so I didn't mind. Lee and I were madly in love and that was enough. We were completely optimistic about the future, sharing a little apartment sparsely filled with second hand furniture. I had never been happier. By the time the marriage ended, four children and fifteen years later, we were living in a large beautiful home full of priceless antiques and I was miserable.

For much of my married life I appeared as a tall blonde in a mink coat, attending premieres on the arm of a move star, famous for my fabulous Hollywood dinner parties, acting the life of the Hollywood wife to the fullest. Few knew about the roller-coaster ride of my marriage to Lee, a Jekyll and Hyde husband who ricocheted between a life of devotion to me and the children and periods of binge drinking and womanizing.

As miserable as I was, I was afraid to cut the cord. What would become of me and our kids? Leaving was so frightening, leaving and not knowing what I was walking into, particularly with Lee's threats to destroy me if I dared to walk away. It took courage and several years of psychoanalysis to put that life behind me, raise my children as a single mother, then go back to graduate school and pursue a career as a painter.

After earning a BFA and MFA in visual art at the Otis Art Institute in 1976, I was enjoying an exciting life in my studio in Venice, with a career full of travel and exhibits. In 1990, I innocently signed away my Venice building and my home, in a bad investment. Being homeless, I was once again forced to employ all my skills to survive. At the low point, my only possessions were my old Chrysler, my dog and my typewriter. I drove up and down the California coast finding food and shelter by working odd jobs. It was very cathartic, banging it all out on the typewriter keys, trying to understand how I got myself into such a mess.

I looked back on my life, being raised by my grandparents in a small river town in Washington State, running away from home at sixteen, traveling alone on the Greyhound bus to California to live with my father, a used car salesman and avid gambler, whom I had seen only once before. He would prove to be the first in a series of the outrageous, unforgettable personalities in my life, some unknown, some famous worldwide, all brought vividly to life in the pages of *Tales of a Hollywood Housewife.*

I have gone from early nothing, to being rich, then being homeless, and on to the real wealth that comes after being cured of the money disease and discovering the true value of a joyful life.

My guide for making art has always been having enough courage to run the high risk of grand fun. Now, at eighty-one, I apply that to life, having as much fun as possible.

I love words and enjoy telling stories. Having a trained eye and ear has been invaluable in seeing scenes and characters and hearing what they have to say.

I can't think of better qualifications for writing. While in the thick of past personal situations, particularly those loaded with adversity, I was writing my thoughts and feelings as therapy. As I learned from those experiences and was able to distance myself from my past I became interested in putting my stories into a book to bring to the reader an honest behind-the-scenes portrait of my life. It has been a rewarding endeavor.

1

Finding Daddy in the Land of Milk and Honey

The Greyhound bus pulled into the Hollywood station. I was a rumpled mess, exhausted from thirty-six hours of trying to shut out the noise of two drunken sailors and curl my long, young body into a comfortable position. I carried my Samsonite suitcase into the waiting room, hoping to recognize the man in the photo, now older and out of uniform. Before running away from my grandparents' house in the small river town of Sedro-Woolley, Washington, in June 1945, I had phoned him at his office, collect, to say I was coming. He was out, so I had left a message. But no one was there to meet me.

My heart sank. Had my father pulled another disappearing act? I searched in my pocket, found his home phone number, resurrected my courage, and called.

"Hello," a sweet-voiced woman answered.

"Is this Hollywood 9141?"

"Yes."

"Is Mr. Ebeling there?"

"Who's calling?"

"Betty . . . his daughter." *Who is she?* I wondered. I tried to pick up pieces of the long, muffled discussion in the background. Finally she returned to the phone and I told her where I was.

"Wait there, honey. I'll be right down."

An hour later a big, buxom, bleached blond in a red-and yellow-flowered jersey dress with plunging neckline, her heavy makeup obvious in the noonday sun, walked in, spotted me, and came right over. We looked at each other in disbelief. I was shocked by her appearance, and she probably had never confronted a skinny, six-foot teenager in saddle shoes and letter sweater. Finally she broke the ice. "Hi, honey, I'm Faye."

Following "Good trip?" and "Fine," we lapsed into an awkward silence. She picked up my suitcase and led me out of the building to a sleek, black Lincoln Continental, double-parked.

My shyness was quickly superseded by fear when Faye, without warning, pulled into heavy traffic. Horns honked and drivers shouted. The car lurched up Sunset as her right foot spasmodically jumped from accelerator to brake, barely avoiding rear-ending the car ahead. Amazingly, we made it to the turnoff for Hollywood Hills without a scratch. The Lincoln swerved up a winding road and pulled into the driveway of a stately Mediterranean mansion.

Daddy's Mediterranean Mansion

Climbing the tile steps to my father's beautiful home, I was sure my Cinderella dreams had come true until a black Chow dog confronted me at the front door. He snarled and I jumped back.

"Down, Oscar!" Faye commanded. She took him upstairs and I was left alone to fend for myself.

I timidly wandered from the garishly furnished sunken living room into the formal dining room. From there I discovered a room with a bar, jukebox, slot machine, pool table, and the first TV I had ever seen. I went into the kitchen and peered into the refrigerator. It was empty except for a carton of milk and an uncovered plate of dried-out cold cuts and Swiss cheese, dominated by the smell of a dill pickle.

After what seemed an eternity, Faye came into the living room, where I was sitting on the edge of a gold velvet sofa. As though announcing an audience with the Wizard of Oz, she said, "He will see you now." I stood; panic grabbed my stomach and I thought I was going to throw up right there on the Oriental rug.

"Go on up," she said, pointing the way. "I have to get his medicine."

I went up the stairs and down a long hallway leading to the master suite. I peered through the bedroom door. There he was, my savior, bigger and more handsome than I had imagined, stretched out on ivory satin pillows, sporting blue silk monogrammed pajamas and a giant hangover. He rolled over and looked me up and down.

"How ya doin', kiddo?" he said with a wink.

"Fine, thank you." I was too tongue-tied to say more. Faye hurried in with a bottle of Pepto-Bismol. He turned to her as she ladled a tablespoon of the pink, pasty liquid into his mouth.

"She's got my nose, don't you think?" he asked Faye. Then he turned back to me. "Well, you're here. How long you planning to stay?"

"Daddy," I stammered, the word feeling strange in my mouth. We'd never spoken in person before. "Don't you remember?" I extended my sweaty palm and showed him my treasured photo of him, creased from two years of being tucked nightly under my pillow back home in Washington.

He studied it quickly. "I looked pretty good in a uniform." He smiled.

"Read the back," I implored him. "You said I could come live with you. You said I could go to UCLA."

He turned it over and read the words he had inscribed to me. To my horror, he seemed amused.

"You're a funny kid. How old are you?"

"Sixteen."

How did you ever get all the way to California? Your Grandma and Grandpa know you're here?"

"I left them a note."

"Oh, boy. I'm not their favorite person, you know."

"It will be okay. I swear."

He looked up at me, and this time I managed to hold his gaze. *You can't send me all the way back there. Please.*

3

"So, okay." My father took a breath and let it out in a whistle. "UCLA. It's as good as it gets—your Daddy ought to know."

"You're right," I said. "They're starting a new music department."

"Music? First things first, kiddo. Let's think about your sorority. It's Delta Delta Delta for you, Aunt Rella's sorority, probably the best sorority on campus. That way you'll meet all the right people. If we're lucky you'll get pinned to a young man from the best fraternity, get married, and we'll all live happily ever after." He laughed, wheezed, then sank back into his pillows with a moan.

"Well, that's it, kiddo. Faye, show her the guest room." Oscar followed me back down the hall, growling.

After spending a few hours behind closed doors of the master suite, my father appeared in a tan suit, white silk tie, and brown and white spectator shoes. It was three in the afternoon and he was ready to start his day. He told Faye to take care of me and get me ready for my coming out. Then he jumped into a sports car that resembled a space ship and sped off. I couldn't imagine what my father did to be so rich and powerful.

Daddy

Faye made a grocery run to the local deli. After a dinner of a bologna sandwich, potato chips, and a Coke, I went to my chintz bedroom, crawled between the pink sheets, and longed for Grandma's cooking.

The next day Faye and I drove down Sunset Boulevard to attend the Sunday church service at Aimee Semple McPherson's Evangelical Temple. As soon as we walked into the round, white building, Faye went into the first pew, fell on her knees, and began to pray. She looked up after a few minutes. "I'm very religious," she whispered shyly.

Aimee made her entrance onto the stage wearing a long, flowing, white robe. She bore a striking resemblance to Faye, with long blond curls and heavy makeup. After a lively hymn from the large choir, accompanied by a brass band and clapping, Aimee talked about having been carried away by the devil. "My Lord Jesus brought me back to you . . . you, my loyal, God-fearing followers." The congregation added *amens* and applause.

Faye gave me a sideway glance. "You been baptized?" I nodded. "Good. Otherwise you're going to hell."

When the service was over, our next stop downtown was Clifton's Cafeteria. We entered through double swinging doors and walked past a scenic landscape with a mountaintop chapel nestled in the redwoods and a few deer peering shyly from behind the trees. I got into the buffet line.

"You gotta try the jello," Faye advised. "My favorite is the yellow because sometimes it has a piece of pear inside!"

On our way to a table Faye pointed to the wall. "A deer used to hang right up there. I guess they moved him. Now they've got a chicken and a crow. Let's sit here by the moose head."

When we arrived at my father's car lot, the first thing I saw was a billboard of Daddy himself, in Indian headdress, looming over a sign that said, "Chief Ernie's: A Solid Block of Solid Cars."

Faye looked up with pride at that sign. "Do you know your father is the biggest used car dealer in L.A.?"

"Really?"

Pre-war, used cars lined the block as far as the eye could see.

"All these are his," she said as we pulled into the lot.

I looked through a window of the office and saw an older black man shaking his fist. The man stormed out yelling, "You cheatin' son of a bitch!" He got into a beat-up blue Chevrolet coupe and the car sputtered off, steam pouring out from under the hood.

Daddy came out of his office and turned to a salesman. "That guy thinks he should get his money back. Fat chance. Keep him off my lot."

"Right, Chief," the salesman responded.

Daddy turned to Faye and me, all smiles. "Why don't you girls go across the street to the bar? I'll be over in a few minutes."

I had never been to a bar. As we left the bright sunshine and entered The HotSpot, a dark, neighborhood watering hole, I could barely see the few shady-looking men giving us the once-over. Nat King Cole's "Route 66" blared from the jukebox as we sat on a couple of bar stools. Faye ordered a Coke for herself and a Shirley Temple for me.

A few minutes later Daddy arrived and seemed to know everyone in the place. He sidled up to the bar, ordered a double martini, straight up, with two olives, put his arm around me, and called out, "Hey, everybody. I want you to meet my niece." They smiled and waved. I played dumb. When his drinking buddies went back to their Liar's dice, my father looked at me, winked, and whispered, "You don't mind, do you, kiddo? I'm too young to have a daughter your age."

Daddy called the bartender over and ordered drinks for everyone. "By the way, Johnny," he added, "I want to place a bet. A hundred bucks on Baby Girl to win in the fourth."

"Ernie, you're already over your limit. Freddy says you owe him. Time to settle up."

"Come on. I'm good for it. This is a hot tip."

We spent the rest of the afternoon waiting for my father to finish his cocktails. Each time we were ready to leave, another pal arrived and bought a round. I had three Shirley Temples lined up in front of me when we finally made our exit. He left his sports car on the lot and insisted on driving the Lincoln Continental down Sunset Boulevard to Earl Carroll's nightclub. On the way, he turned on the radio and switched the dial.

"Listen to this, kiddo. This is my show."

"You have a show?" Wild ecstatic voices, praising God in harmony, filled the car.

"Yours truly, Chief Ernie, is the big sponsor of the Gospel Hour. I'm no dummy! Every nigger in town gets his car from me."

We pulled up in front of a neon sign proclaiming, "Through these portals pass the most beautiful girls in the world." The valet raced to open the car doors, greeting my father by name.

Everyone from the manager to the hatcheck girl knew my father. He slipped the maître d' a wad of bills for a ringside table. The pretty, barely-clad cigarette girl seemed happy to see Daddy, and the waiter brought him a drink as soon as we were seated at our table. He ordered porterhouse steaks, baked potatoes, and salads for the three of us—but never ate a bite the whole evening, preferring to drink his dinner. I was already feasting on the thrill of being in a real nightclub, like the ones I had seen in the movies. Jimmy Durante was on stage with the showgirls delivering very suggestive adlibs. My father was the perfect audience, laughing loudly and clapping nonstop. "Jimmy's a friend of mine. This is as good as it gets, right, kiddo?" I agreed. Durante spotted my father and came over to our table after the first show. Once again Daddy introduced me as his niece.

Daddy, Faye, and I at Earl Carroll's nightclub 1945

* * *

My father was nothing like I had imagined. I had seen him only once during my childhood, on his singular visit to his wealthy family in Burlington, five miles from where I lived with my mother's parents, Grandma and Grandpa Rundquist.

Waiting with my brother, Dickey, to meet Daddy, 1937

His sister, my aunt Rella, was there, which made his pending arrival less stressful. I loved Rella, decked out in her outlandish costume jewelry and bleached bobbed hairdo. She was a light in my childhood—always had treats and hugs for me, and when we were together, she made me feel important, listened to, and acknowledged.

Aunt Rella

"You look adorable!" she exclaimed that afternoon, whirling me around in the pink taffeta dress she'd bought for the occasion. "He'll love you." Rella bit her lip and corrected herself. "He already does, honey."

When my father walked through the door, I wanted to look at him, to take him in. Instead, I found myself distracted by the presence of a strange woman who hung on his arm. She didn't say much to our family, and we didn't say much to her. At one point she took out a mother-of-pearl compact and checked her lipstick. My father was there so briefly he was more of a shadow than a man. I don't think we spoke. He kissed my cheek and then disappeared.

"Come on, baby, let's have some cake," Aunt Rella said as soon as he was gone, hustling me into the kitchen, where the chocolate cake she'd baked for the occasion sat untouched. "Then I'll play some ragtime."

Rella was a bright, talented concert pianist who had paid for her education by playing for silent movies. Listening to Rella on the piano always made me want to sing and dance.

"Do you think he'll come back?" I found the nerve to ask a little while later, my mouth full of cake.

"My brother's a strange man," said Rella. "I couldn't have left you to begin with." Then she changed the subject.

I often wished I were Rella's child. Years later, I found out she had felt the same. Although she had two children of her own, she had wanted to adopt me, but my mother wouldn't allow it, despite having left me to be raised by her parents. Aunt Rella always let me know she felt a special connection to me. She saw in me something nobody else in my scattered upbringing seemed to notice—perhaps a talent, or a spark of intelligence, I never knew. I just knew I had someone in my corner.

The rest of my father's family made me feel like the poor relative, which, in truth, I was. My mother's parents, Grandma and Grandpa Rundquist, had no use for them, given my father's early abandonment of my older brother, Dickey, and myself; but we were permitted, for some reason, to see our other grandparents, and we spent much of our childhoods being shuffled back and forth between the two families. Wherever I was, I felt like a traitor to the other.

My father's mother, Grandma Ebeling, was a strict German Lutheran who put the fear of God into anyone who crossed her path. Her three-story Victorian house, where she reigned over church socials and large gatherings like a queen, was furnished with beautiful antiques, Oriental rugs, and fine paintings. A well-educated, accomplished painter, tailor, cook, and musician, she took it upon herself to tutor me in piano. She wasn't any fun, but the time I spent with her changed my perception of the world.

On many Saturday mornings she would come to get me in a long, black Packard touring sedan wearing a hat, gloves, mink paw stole, and a dour expression, and I would ride off into my other life.

Over one particular Christmas with the extended Ebeling family, I shared my cousin Barbara's bedroom. She had a white carpet, pink floral wallpaper, and drapes to match. I lay on one of the two canopied beds with ruffled chintz spreads and matching pillow shams listening to Barbara's chattering on about her private school, summer camp, and what fun it was to cruise through the San Juan Islands, but I couldn't take my eyes off her mouth. Braces! I had been to a dentist only once in my life. Those metal wires over her teeth summed up everything she had that I was missing.

I didn't like my father's family, but I wanted what they had.

Aunt Rella and I didn't mention my father again for a long time. But one afternoon she mentioned casually that she'd heard my father was living in Bellingham, an hour from my home.

"What's he doing there?" I asked, looking at myself in the mirror. I loved the clothes Aunt Rella gave me. It was the only time I'd get new things rather than hand-me-downs.

"He's a sign painter, sweetie—here, let me fix that collar—he has a business making outdoor ads."

That image must have been buried in my mind, for not long afterward, I was walking down the street when I noticed a sign on the side of a parked truck: "Sunset Outdoor Advertising." I was sure, very sure, that I was looking at my father's truck. I imagined waiting around to surprise him when he came back from wherever he was. I could still envision the scene as I walked on by, not looking back. I never heard a word from my father until I was fourteen.

Out of the blue, an envelope arrived. He had sent me a birthday card, although it wasn't my birthday. Inside was a photograph of himself in an army uniform and a note. I memorized it. "Hi, kiddo. After your Daddy wins the war, you'll come live with me in sunny California. I'll send you to UCLA, the best college in the world." I put his picture under my pillow and studied it every night. He resembled a blond Clark Gable.

"Come live with me in sunny California." I repeated those words to myself silently as I worked secretly to impress him, even though we were not really in contact. I practiced the piano two hours a day, playing everything from Bach to boogie-woogie. I sang my heart out in the school chorus. I taught myself every popular dance step, tapping and jitterbugging my way to local fame. I graduated early, at sixteen, from Sedro-Woolley High, earning four stripes and three stars for sports, which I proudly wore on my letter sweater. I was full of ambition, ready to take on the world and ready to greet the man of my dreams, my father.

*   *   *

2

Look at Me, Playing Dress-Up for Rushing

If you were a coed in 1945, you probably wore a pleated skirt, a blouse with a Peter Pan collar, and maybe a cardigan with pearl buttons. Not me. On my first day at UCLA I showed up in my bright blue and gold letter sweater with an *SW* for Sedro-Woolley High School. I didn't get very far when I greeted the girls click-clacking in their perfect penny loafers up and down the halls. They just responded with amused indifference and quickly moved on. The only exception was Beverly Dixon, whom I met on the bus going to campus. She was cute, friendly, and seemed to know everyone on campus. I was grateful to her for introducing me to her pals. Also, my social life was hopefully being worked out for me by my father, who'd set me up to join his sister's sorority, Tri Delt, one of the most popular at UCLA. I went home and told Daddy I needed new clothes, particularly an outfit for the first day of "rushing," where I would meet my Tri Delt "sisters."

"That's Faye's department, kiddo," he said, not looking up from his racing form. The horses were serious business for my father.

"I'll take you shopping, honey," said Faye. "I know all the best stores. You leave it to me."

So off we went to Frederick's of Hollywood.

I stood on front of the store window blushing at the sight of almost naked mannequins wearing teeny sequined panties and spangled, hot pink halter tops zipped down to there. There was nothing like Frederick's in the little town where I'd grown up. I don't think anyone in Sedro-Woolley had ever seen a push-up bra.

"Aren't they gorgeous?" Faye sighed.

We went in and I looked around in amazement. There were plastic pink torsos sporting brassieres that looked like torpedoes ready to fire. "Look at this skirt!" Faye gushed, handling a piece of sequined fabric the size of a hankie, the hem dripping with feathers.

"Faye, I don't think—," I began, but she was off to grab a salesgirl.

After an hour of makeover madness, I was all decked out in a skintight, deeply low-cut, black rayon cocktail dress, perfect for showing off the breasts and hips I didn't have. Falsies forced on me helped the upper half. My long, skinny legs were covered in black stockings with seams that defied being straight, and my feet were crammed into black patent four-inch high heels. As a final touch, Faye had added a pillbox black hat with a little, black Swiss polka-dot veil. Swaying on my heels, barely able to see through the veil, I faced myself in the mirror. Faye had painted my lips with her favorite Flaming Coral lipstick.

"You're almost there," she purred, looking at me admiringly.

Faye was suddenly squealing. "Ooooh! Lookit *that!*" as she dashed across the room, practically dragging the salesgirl with her.

"Oh, this is *perfect!*" Faye beamed, back at my side. "Hold out your hands." I extended my arms, encased in slinky, elbow-length black gloves. Faye slid a rhinestone the size of a golf ball onto my left ring finger. It sent out blinding, shimmering lights. *This can't be happening*, I kept thinking. "You're gonna knock 'em dead, honey," she said in a hushed tone. "You look real . . . elegant."

That night I modeled my new look for Daddy and he, in his cups, said, "Ya look swell, kiddo," then turned his attention back to Oscar, sitting in his lap, whom he was attempting to hypnotize.

The first rushing invitation was for Saturday afternoon tea. My father sent me off alone to drive his black Lincoln Continental from one end of Sunset to the other, all the way to the campus. I wanted to leave the car as far away as possible from the Tri Delt house so no one there could witness my many attempts to parallel park. I finally left the monster on a side street, two feet from the curb. I teetered awkwardly up the block in my patent leather high heels, the underarms of my black dress wet with sweat.

I rang the doorbell while trying to adjust my veil, which was fluttering in the light breeze, tickling my nose. A trim little sorority girl in a navy blue skirt and crisp white blouse, buttoned all the way to the top, opened

13

the door to welcome me. The high heels made me six foot, two inches, putting my pointy, fake breasts in line with her nose. We both stood there open-mouthed, staring at each other.

"Can I help you?" she asked, her voice overly sweet.

I managed to explain who I was, and she, attempting to be gracious, invited me into the empty formal dining room. I was unfashionably early and therefore the only pledge in the room, surrounded by Tri Delts in their pastel cashmeres and single strands of pearls. I stepped in and was greeted by complete silence.

I sat down in a chair against the wall and crossed my seam-stockinged legs, trying to smile and speak, but all of the girls had turned away from me and were talking to each other. Eventually other properly dressed pledges began to arrive, each one coming in, introducing herself in a most genteel fashion, giving me a glance, then happily joining the proper party.

High tea was served. Balancing the cup and saucer on my lap, I took my first bite of a petit four, forgetting the veil covering my mouth. Crumbs fell everywhere. In a desperate move to be casual, I brushed the crumbs onto the plush rug, lifted my veil, and sipped my tea. One of the sorority girls passed a silver box of cigarettes. Never having smoked, I took one, lit up, inhaled, and had a horrendous coughing spasm. I hacked away as bridge tables were being set up. Called over to play, I removed my gloves, put my rhinestone back on, and dealt. I did fairly well until I got the bid and had no idea how to play the hand. Under the table, I slipped the rhinestone ring into my bag.

"I've lost my diamond!" I cried, holding up my left hand for all to see. Then I jumped up and ran out the door.

"Well, that's it for Tri Delt," I sighed. Alone in the car, I cried all the way home, feeling the sting of mascara for the first time.

3

Alone on My Own in L.A.

The following week the Tri Delts spotted me having lunch in the commissary with two classmates—Joanne Davis, a bright, sophisticated Jewish girl from Brooklyn, and Bill Duffy, a black scholarship student from Inglewood. The cute hostess from rushing strolled over.

"Betty, could you come with me? We'd like to talk to you." The Tri Delt table fell silent as we approached. Tammy, the sorority president, pointed to a chair. "Why don't you sit with us?"

"I'm sitting with my friends," I said.

"Now that you're a Tri Delt pledge, it's important whom you're seen with."

"I don't understand."

"It's very simple. Our sorority is closed."

"Closed?"

"We do not take Jews and Negroes," a sorority sister said.

Tammy hushed her and took over. "You realize, don't you, because of a legacy we had to take you in." I was taken aback. I got up to leave as she continued. "And another thing—you forgot to follow the dress code." I hadn't bothered reading the booklet given me earlier in the week. "We don't want you wearing that letter sweater anymore. We wear pastel cashmeres over blouses with Peter Pan collars." The Tri Delt look-alikes nodded simultaneously.

I shook my head in disbelief and walked away. As I made my way back to Joanne and Bill, I made eye contact with one of the guys sitting with the Sigma Alpha Epsilon fraternity, behind the Tri Delts. He was a beautiful sight. And he smiled at me. That took some of the sting out of my brief encounter with the Peter Pan Collars.

Back at the commissary for lunch the next day, I could feel cool air on the back of my neck as I passed by and purposefully ignored the Tri Delt table. Sitting down with Joanne and Bill, I heard a voice at my shoulder almost as soon as I picked up my sandwich.

"Why aren't you with your sorority sisters?"

I turned and saw the handsome guy I'd spotted at the SAE table. He sat down next to me.

"Ha. I've been disowned," I told him. "Are you allowed to fraternize with a 'Non-Org'?"

"I'll take my chances," he smiled, extending his hand to me. "Nice to meet you, Miss Non-Org. I'm Jerry Rogers."

Jerry and I had an almost instantaneous friendship. We shared a mutual love of music and would hang out on campus before my voice classes and sing show tunes together. He'd drive me home and we'd sit there, parked, singing obscure musical numbers in harmony. Acoustics are great in a parked car.

"You've really got a great voice, Betty," he said one afternoon. "There's a friend of mine you've got to meet. Come to a party with me tonight?"

"Sure," I said, getting out of the car.

"I'll pick you up at nine," Jerry called after me, "and dig out a party dress!"

I borrowed my pal Joanne's black beaded sweater to wear with my white sharkskin pleated skirt and black patent heels.

"Wow, Jerry, who lives here?" I said as we pulled up to a beautiful Mediterranean estate in the Pacific Palisades overlooking the sea.

"Roger Edens. I've known him forever. You'll love him."

"What's not to love?" I said as we entered the elegant home furnished in perfect taste, full of beautiful people. The party was in full swing.

There was a crowd drinking and smoking around the open bar, others laughing and chatting on low sofas, and another group gathered around a grand piano singing. Jerry, a couple of drinks in, joined them.

"Betty! Get over here!"

I made my way through the crowd to the Steinway.

"Come on, honey, just pretend we're in my car," Jerry teased, cajoling me into joining him in one of our favorites, "We're a Couple of Swells." We got a round of applause, and the refined gentleman who had accompanied us looked up and smiled, still noodling the keys.

"Hey, Roger," Jerry greeted him, "this is my friend I was telling you about." Roger began chords leading into the verse of "But Not for Me" in my mezzo soprano key and encouraged me to join him. I didn't know then that I was singing for the head music producer at MGM, the genius behind Judy Garland and Lena Horne. I probably would have blown it if I had known. Instead, I just let loose. When the song ended and the applause died down, Roger took my hand and led me to the bar. He poured each of us a glass of champagne and tipped his glass. "I'd like to coach you."

After that night my life revolved around my classical music studies at UCLA and working with Roger, who brought out a different side of my singing. We became easy friends, and one evening I found myself sitting at a table in the Club Gala on Sunset with Jerry, Roger, and Lena Horne, listening to Bobby Short. Lena, looking beautiful in a black picture hat, got up, leaned between two Steinway Grand pianos, and sang "Stormy Weather" while Bobby played. Later we all went to Lena's house in the hills. Bobby played piano, and I sang "Little Girl Blue," and "Last Night When We Were Young" while Lena Horne danced.

To hell with the Tri-Delts. I was in heaven.

After the Tri-Delts had given me their final warning, I returned home from school one afternoon and could not get Daddy's black hearse of a car into the garage, so I parked on the street in front of the house. I opened the front door and was confronted by Daddy in a rage. "What the hell's goin' on at school?" he shouted. "Hangin' out with kikes and niggers!" He waved a letter from the Delta Delta Delta Sorority in my face. "Well, no Tri Delt for you, kiddo."

Through the bay window, behind his back, I saw his Lincoln slip away from the curb and coast down the street. Daddy, oblivious, carried on.

"You come down here and turn my world upside down. No daughter of mine is gonna' ruin my good name. I'm Chief Ernie. Everybody knows me. I've got my reputation to think about. I don't need this."

I held my breath as the car gathered speed.

"You've made a fine mess of things. What more could possibly happen to ruin my day?"

The loud crash got his attention. I froze. He turned and saw his Lincoln imbedded in the neighbor's house on the corner.

The Tri Delts threw me out of their house and my father threw me out of his. I decided then to get a part-time job and make it on my own. The enrollment at UCLA jumped from eight thousand to fifteen thousand at the end of the war in 1945 and there was little housing available, so Joanne and I put our names on the waiting list for a dorm room and moved into the Starlight Motel in Santa Monica. Joanne received a monthly allowance from her loving family in New York and offered to pay the rent until I started working. I wrote to Grandma Ebeling, who had promised to loan me money for school if I needed it. She wrote back telling me if I really wanted to go to college I would find a way. Thankfully, UCLA granted me a scholarship when the school learned of my situation.

Despite the turmoil of my life outside of school, I loved my music classes, particularly my daily voice lesson with Erv, and the new friendships I made in the very first music and theare departments on campus. It was fun arranging songs for the musical comedies being produced by the students. Jerry and I continued to keep constant company, and together we had built up quite a collection of those little known torch songs that pull at the heart strings.

The more time I spent with Jerry, the more those love songs began to eat at me. He was so handsome, so much fun, and he seemed to adore me. I certainly knew how I felt about him. Why didn't he ever make a move? Finally, I got up my nerve. *Maybe he's just shy,* I thought. We finished a duet, and I reached over and gently touched his leg. I moved in, hoping he'd respond with a kiss. Instead, he pulled away. I felt like sinking into a hole. He must have seen the look on my face, because he took my hand.

"Betty, I love you. You know that."

You don't do anything about it, I thought, but said nothing.

"Look, I've got to tell you something. I like guys."

"What does that mean?" I said. I hadn't a clue.

"Do you remember the Kinsey Report?"

I had to have it spelled out for me. When at last I understood, I said, "Well, I'm adding you to my list of things I've been deprived of until now—blacks, Jews, and boys who like other boys."

We laughed, hugged, and promised friendship forever, but it was a long time before I could look at Jerry without thinking,—*If only . . .*

4

Innocence Lost: Learning Life's Lessons

As the semester was coming to a close at UCLA and Christmas approached, I still hadn't heard from Daddy. I knew my roommate, Joanne, hated living in our dank room at the Starlight Motel, so I tried to make the place look more cheerful. She came back from school to find me hanging Christmas ornaments in our abode to detract from the water-stained walls in the dreary room. The peeling paper on one wall was hidden behind stacked wooden boxes full of school books and a clothes rack full of her many outfits. Joanne sighed.

"It's not that bad," I said.

"Not that bad," she moaned. "What a dump!"

"It's only temporary," I said. "I'll pay my half of the rent as soon as I get a job."

She looked out into the cement parking lot and went to pull down the shade. It came off the roller. "Oh, shit," she said as she grabbed a dingy white towel from the bathroom to hang over the window.

A couple of days before the school break, Joanne was in class and our friend Bill came over to study with me for an exam. While he was using the bathroom I heard a knock at the door. I opened it and saw Daddy standing there, beaming in a Santa Claus hat and dangling car keys from one hand. "Ho, ho, ho! Merry Christmas, kiddo."

"Daddy. What a surprise . . . You're not mad anymore?"

"No. You think I could stay mad at my little girl? Santa's brought you a Christmas present." Behind him Faye was standing next to a '36 Hudson Terraplane with a huge red ribbon attached to the hood. She waved. Daddy's roadster was parked next to the clunker. "You didn't think I'd forget my little girl, did you?"

The toilet flushed and Daddy's face fell as Bill appeared, stepped forward, and extended his hand. "Bill Duffy, sir. Merry Christmas."

Daddy ignored the greeting and glared at Bill. "What are you doing here?" He looked at me in disbelief. "You're living with a schwartze? Well, that beats all." He tossed me the keys and turned to leave, calling to Faye, "Get in the car." He jumped into the driver's seat next to her and raced away.

Before I could close the door the short, fat, bald motel manager blocked the entrance. "Well, this is a pretty picture," he sneered. He raised his fist to Bill. "I could have you arrested. We run a respectable place here. Get off my property, pronto!" Then he turned to me. "And you, you little tramp, shacking up with a jiggaboo. Get your ass out of here before I call the police."

After Bill took off, I loaded our belongings into the Hudson and drove past the office. The manager was standing out front with his arms folded. I yelled, "You creep!" and stepped on the gas, almost hitting Joanne, who was coming up the walk. I pulled over.

"Get in," I said. Joanne did, and smoke poured from the exhaust as we sped up Pico Boulevard. "The nerve of that guy," I muttered.

Joanne calmly lit a Camel cigarette. "Will you please tell me what's going on?"

"The manager accused me of shacking up with Bill. Threw us out."

"Big deal," she said. "I've been thrown out of better places than that. Where'd you get this old jalopy?"

"Christmas present from Daddy."

"That was nice of him."

"Nice! He also thinks I'm carrying on with Bill. Men's minds must be in the gutter . . . What's a schwartze?"

Joanne looked at me and laughed. "What an innocent!" The car started missing, then sputtered and died in the middle of heavy rush hour traffic. Horns honked as I tried frantically to start the engine. "Some present," I moaned. Finally moving again, we rattled on in my old heap of a car, looking for a different motel to call home. We were passing one dive after another, many of them sparsely decorated with blinking holiday lights for the season, making me feel even more blue.

Joanne glanced over at me. "Cheer up," she said, lighting another cigarette. "We're going to Bogie's for Christmas dinner." I gave her a questioning look.

"Bogie . . . Humphrey Bogart. My cousin's husband?"

I remembered then that Lauren Bacall was Joanne's first cousin. It wasn't the type of thing Joanne would mention often. She could have cared less about stardom and fame.

"The pool there is great. We'll bring our suits and live the life of luxury." She smiled at me as we pulled into the rundown Do Drop Inn, with a "Vacancy" sign in neon orange. Our new home.

A few days later I called my father. We hadn't spoken since our scene at the motel.

"Hi, Daddy," I said nervously

"Hey, kiddo! How's my girl?"

"It's good to talk to you, Daddy. I'm glad you're not upset."

"No. All's forgiven. Daddy loves you. It's Christmas! Why don't you come to Tijuana with Faye and me? Daddy will show you a good time at the track."

"I can't. Actually, I'm going to Humphrey Bogart's."

"You're going to Humphrey Bogart's? And I'm going to the moon!"

"I'm not making it up. My roommate, Joanne, is Lauren Bacall's cousin."

"Huh. I didn't know Lauren Bacall was Jewish," he said.

"We'll come by Christmas morning before you leave for Tijuana. I have a little present for you."

On Christmas day Thomas, Humphrey Bogart's black, effeminately gay, and well-mannered chauffeur, came to fetch us. I grabbed my beach bag and jumped into the back seat of a silver Cadillac, pinching myself as we glided through Beverly Hills. Joanne directed Thomas into the hills of Silver Lake for a quick visit with Daddy.

"Thanks for making this stop, Joanne. I know it's out of the way."

"No problem. I've been dying to meet the chief."

We pulled into the drive of my father's glamorous house.

"Wow," said Joanne. "I guess gambling pays off.

Daddy, peering out the window, was equally impressed by the silver caddy out front. He and Faye greeted us eagerly as we came in the door and I introduced Joanne.

Faye took us immediately to view her masterpiece—an artificial Christmas tree covered with blue lights and plastic angels. "How do you like it?"

Joanne was speechless. I mumbled, "Wonderful."

"This is the best invention ever," said Faye. "You never have to buy another."

Daddy cornered Joanne. "I hear you're Lauren Bacall's cousin.

Joanne smiled. "Yes."

"How did that happen?" Daddy said.

"My mother and her mother, Nat, are sisters."

"How old is she? She can't be much older than you. Did you two grow up together?"

"Yes. In New York." I could see Joanne wanted to escape, but no such luck.

Daddy was unstoppable. "Is she as sexy in person as she is on the screen? I'll never forget her, 'You know how to whistle, don't you? Just pucker up and blow.'" He let out a laugh.

Joanne looked desperate, so I went to her rescue.

"Sorry, we have to run. Merry Christmas to you both. Have a good time in Tijuana."

After hugs and kisses, Joanne and I went on our way up Benedict Canyon to the Cape Cod home nestled in the hills. An authentic Christmas tree stood inside the entrance, decorated with real candles. Boughs of greens were draped on the beams, and carols played throughout the house. I thought this home would be more like those in the movies, but it was no bigger than my father's place in Silver Lake. It was comfortably furnished in traditional Early American design, although the occupants were certainly not your traditional couple. Bogie was fifty-six when he married Betty, Lauren Bacall, who was only nineteen. No wonder Bogie called her "Baby."

No one was there to greet us, but Joanne paid no notice. She knew her way around. We went out to the cabana, put on our swimsuits, jumped into the pool, and grabbed a couple of rubber rafts. Shy and insecure, I was relieved in a way not to meet my hosts on arriving.

"How's your love life?" I asked Joanne as we floated. "Are you seeing that disc jockey?"

"Great lover," she said.

"Joanne, he's married."

"Not really," she said. "His wife's frigid. They haven't had sex in years."

"His kids are older than you."

"Can I help it if there's a thirty-year-old woman stuck in this seventeen-year-old body?"

She drifted to the other end of the pool.

I squinted my eyes against the sun and glanced over at Joanne. We were devoted friends and yet so different. She was the kind of girl I never would have associated with in high school. She smoked, drank, and had sex with anyone who turned her on. I now had met my own handsome heartthrob, Bob Horton, who was studying acting in the theater department. But I had to first feel "engaged" to even consider having sex with him, though I wanted him desperately. Also I knew Bob had other girlfriends and I was afraid if I did not eventually "go all the way" he would stop seeing me. The situation had me under a lot of stress.

I was fascinated by Joanne. She was bright, sophisticated, and an excellent student. Above and beyond her promiscuity, she was also very moral and had a strong conviction of her beliefs. She had been raised by her loving family in New York to be honest and forthright. Her father, an attorney, was a liberal politician and Joan followed in his footsteps to the extent of passing out political fliers at the University bus stop. Just being in her company was an eye-opener for me. And I couldn't quite take in her cousin, marrying a movie star thirty-seven years her senior.

"Virgin Marys," Thomas said, lowering the silver tray onto a poolside table.

Joanne and I got out of the pool. She took one of the drinks to the bar and added a shot of vodka. She held out her glass and made a toast to me. "Here's to losing your virginity. Want a shot?"

Dinner was announced, and in we went. I finally met our host and hostess when they came to the table for the traditional turkey feast, joined by Lauren's mother, Nat. Bogie was pleasant, but Lauren and her mother, Joanne's aunt, were cold and unfriendly. They practically ignored my presence. I was uncomfortable, but I had been well trained as a child and spoke only when spoken to. Perhaps my silence and not feeling particularly welcome was a hangover from childhood. Joanne was very much at ease and behaved as if Lauren and she were more than cousins. They were friends. After all, Lauren was only four years older.

As it happened, Christmas day was also Bogie's birthday. He celebrated with many drinks and went on to dominate most of the dinner conversation, finally stopping to ask, "Where's Thomas?"

"He went down the hill for a bottle of milk." Bacall responded.

Bogie was amused. "Well, we won't see him for a few days." He leaned in toward me with a sly grin. "When he's feeling horny, he always says he's going out for milk. He gets drunk, goes cruising, and ends up with some fag. I don't give a damn except when he takes the Caddie." He laughed and downed his drink. I smiled, thinking of Jerry's possible plights.

After dinner Bogie locked himself into his green and red plaid "mad room" to take a nap. Lauren had cleverly mounted a large, sexy portrait of herself on the ceiling over his sofa, so he never stayed mad long. Shortly afterward he ambled out and disappeared to his boat, the *Santana*, anchored in San Pedro. He called Lauren continuously from there and she didn't seem to mind. Obviously, it was some game they played.

Thomas surprised us by returning sober and drove us back to our rundown motel room late in the evening, our arms loaded down with delectable leftovers. We lived off of Bogie's Christmas dinner for the rest of the week. I didn't call Daddy after the holidays, and he didn't call me.

Months later, Joanne and I moved into a UCLA dormitory for a semester and then into the Beverly Glen cottage we would share with my friend Beverly. The three of us had a wonderful time living in the Glen for the next couple of years. I'd become seriously involved with my boyfriend, Bob. He had given me his friendship ring to wear as a symbol of our supposed upcoming engagement. The ring, for both of us, basically acted as a sanction for being lovers. But Bob, being an actor, decided to give New York a shot. So we parted in 1948, with his promise of sending for me as soon as he was settled.

5

The Strange New World of a Hollywood Nanny

I was twenty, just out of college, and training for the opera with my voice teacher Erv. My four years at UCLA as a music major studying voice had flown by. I had wonderful friends, including Robert Walker. While I was working part-time at the Bureau of Occupations on campus, an ad came in seeking an assistant to Lew Wasserman, head of MCA, the biggest talent agency in the business. I thought of Robert and tucked the notice away until I could tell him about it. He got the job.

My good friend Robert Walker

Several months later I was job hunting and he returned the favor. Joan Crawford, one of MCA's clients, needed a nanny. Robert heard about it and called me. He even offered to drive me to the interview on his lunch hour. My nerves were rattling.

"Joanne knows all the Hollywood gossip and said this woman is a *lunatic*," I said. "Did you know she bought these kids? She couldn't adopt them because she wasn't maried."

"Juicy Hollywood gossip. Check it out for yourself and tell me all about it," Robert offered calmly.

"I don't think I'm qualified."

"Tell her you've worked as a camp counselor," he said, laughing. "That should be more than enough for her. She's got four kids. Wouldn't that make any woman desperate for help?"

When we arrived in Brentwood I was so caught up with planning what to say in the interview that I didn't notice when Robert slowed down to come to a stop. *She won't hire me,* I thought. *This is just ridiculous.*

"We're here," said Robert.

I looked up. We were parked in front of an enormous, walled-in, white colonial mansion, larger than any home I'd ever seen. It sat well behind a large, well-tended front garden. Robert looked at his watch. I didn't move.

"I'll be waiting for you around the corner when you're finished," Robert said as I got out of the car.

I opened the gate and walked up the long, brick path to the front door. A tall, mature, slightly fey butler stood waiting for me.

"Yes?"

"Betty Ebeling to see Miss Crawford."

"She's expecting you. This way."

I followed as he led me past circular stairs down a long hallway. En route I spied a white, formal drawing room on my right and an elegant, glassed-in dining area on the left. A hall door swung open and a short, rotund, orange-haired woman in a white uniform poked her head through and gave me the once-over, then disappeared.

"She'll see you now," the butler said, opening the door at the end of the hall to a large, sunlit, book-lined study. Seated at an oval desk was Joan Crawford. Behind her was a curved bay window through which I could see a large, manicured garden with a rectangular pool. I flinched as she stood and came to greet me. There was little resemblance to her image on screen because she was in shorts and wore no makeup. Even so, she looked glamorous—a woman in her forties, of average height, with short, brown hair, large, green eyes, and great legs.

"Hello, Miss Ebeling," she said warmly, giving me a firm handshake. I had never been formally addressed before. I suddenly felt older. She had my resume set out on her desk. "I see here you were a music major, piano and voice. I like that. All children should sing and play the piano. And you're an athlete? Wonderful. You can teach the twins to swim. I want them water safe."

When I told her I had been a camp counselor, she lit up.

"Perfect! You've had experience with groups of children. You can start tomorrow, so get a good night's sleep tonight. Your salary is $200 a month, room and board. You have every Wednesday and every other Thursday off."

I was speechless. I had figured there would be formalities to go through, references to be checked—*something*. I didn't know at the time her help came and left on a regular basis.

"I'll be leaving for New York the day after tomorrow. I'll be gone for six weeks, shooting my new film," she said casually as she continued scanning my resume.

And I'm going to be left with four kids I don't know from Adam, I thought. *This is so weird.* Crawford suddenly came to a point in my resume and her mouth twitched.

"I see you're still studying voice?"

"Oh, yes, I'm training for the opera."

"That's fine as long as it doesn't interfere with your work here. You can study on your days off. One absolute rule," she continued. "No guests. I had to let the last girl go. Too many gentlemen callers. I don't approve of that sort of thing."

She turned to the butler, who had been waiting like a statue in the corner. "Henry, bring in the children."

He walked out, and I could feel my heart pounding. Miss Crawford turned away from me, back to her desk. I tried to appear nonchalant but attentive, a combination that wasn't working too well as I felt my slip threatening to drop down below my skirt at any minute.

The door opened and the children entered in formation behind Henry: Christina, a big-boned, pretty, blonde ten-year-old girl; her younger brother, Christopher, seven, also large, blonde, and healthy-looking; and Cindy and Cathy, very cute pre-school twins. The four children stood at attention. I tried to make eye contact, but they looked only at their mother.

"Good morning, Children."

"Good morning, Mommy Dearest," they answered in unison. I had no idea at the time this title Crawford insisted on would become so famous.

"Meet your new nanny, Miss Ebeling. We'll call her Missy."

Missy! What the hell? A smile stayed plastered on my face.

"Missy, this is Christina, Christopher, and my twins, Cathy and Cindy." The girls curtsied and Christopher bowed, but they still didn't look at me. Finally Miss Crawford made an almost imperceptible nod to Henry, and he stretched out an arm to indicate I should exit.

"We'll expect you after dinner," she said, as I was about to leave.

"See you then," I replied with inane cheer. Miss Crawford responded with a reserved smile.

"Bye, kids," I managed. No response.

Robert, bless him, was waiting as promised, parked under the shade of a tree reading the actor's trade journal, *Variety*. He looked up as I swung the door open and sat there next to him, out of breath.

"What happened?"

"Please, drive." I felt like Crawford could hear me as long as I was still in the neighborhood.

"I'm sorry if this was a bum lead, Betty," Robert said, glancing over at me.

"It wasn't. I got the job."

"You're kidding! I told you. So, what's she like?"

My breath had returned to normal. "I've never met anyone like her. She's definitely a star—very polite, very proper. Not friendly, I'll tell you that. And those kids! They're like little soldiers. If she told them to drop and give her twenty, I think they'd hit the floor in a heartbeat."

"Well, you must have done something right. She gave you the job on the spot."

"I think she's desperate. She told me to move in *tonight!* Not only that, but she's about to leave for New York. I just don't know what to think."

"Even better. She won't be there. Just you and four little kids in that beautiful house? Piece of cake."

"It's exciting, isn't it?" I said, finally letting myself feel the thrill.

"It's great. I'll pick you up to take you back there at seven. We'll go grab a bite first."

As soon as I got through the door of my Beverly Glen cottage, I began throwing clothes into my suitcase.

"Oh, *no.*" Joanne was standing in my doorway, smoking a cigarette and shaking her head. "Don't tell me."

"I'm moving in there tonight. Come on, Jo, how bad can it be?"

"You know what I say," she said wryly. "No matter how bad you *think* it can be, it can always be worse. Look," she added, reaching for an ashtray, "I know you need to find work, but why there?"

I'd almost finished packing; everything I owned could go into one big suitcase. "It's a lot of money. It's an amazing house. She's gone a lot of the time. I'm just giving it a shot, that's all."

Joanne let out a resigned sigh. "Well, your room will be waiting for you when you're ready to come home."

"I hope I'll come home in a few months with money in my pocket and stories to tell."

"I'll miss you."

"You will not," I laughed. "You'll see me every chance I get, every day off, every *minute* off."

My corner of the shared bedroom looked suddenly bare.

She hugged me hard when it was time for me to go. "Call me when you get one of those minutes off, okay?"

That night in the Crawford home, Henry showed me to my room in the servant's quarters. It wasn't large, but it was private and I had my own bath. After living a cluttered, communal life with Joanne and Bev, I felt pampered to have a real room of my own.

"Marie's room is next door, and I'm down the hall," Henry said. "Miss Crawford will see you after breakfast, which is served at seven sharp." After a hasty "Good night," I was left on my own.

I didn't see the kids that first evening. I unpacked, sat on my bed, and wondered what I should do. I went out into the long hallway but saw and heard no one. The house was silent. I tiptoed back into my little hideaway, set my alarm, and, once in bed, fell into an immediate deep sleep.

The next morning Miss Crawford was nowhere to be seen. I was handed off to Mrs. Brown, an older woman who had been with the household for years. She would be my trainer and would cover for me on my days off. Since it was Saturday, Christina and Christopher were not in school, so they made the rounds with us. We'd spoken very little at breakfast, but Christina was sweet and well behaved, so we seemed to be getting off to a good start.

Mrs. Brown led me first into Cindy and Cathy's bedroom. Everything for the twins was white and perfectly matched; there were huge stuffed animals—two of each—and two little rocking chairs. "Every day you will get them up and dressed for pre-school and breakfast at seven. When they're away you'll change their bed sheets, dust, vacuum, and scrub their bathroom," Mrs. Brown instructed. All that cleaning had never come up in the interview, but, okay. Mrs. Brown was already down the hall and going on to the next bedroom.

Christina and Christopher shared a large room that had once been their nursery. Though Christina was ten and Christopher seven, no attempt had been made to create any privacy between them. Christina was pleased to show off her things: a chintz canopied bed and a closet full of beautiful clothes, hung neatly in a row. Chris hung back dolefully.

"Christina and Christopher are to be up, dressed, and at breakfast on their own, and they take care of their room themselves," Mrs. Brown continued. "You are to check and be sure the clothes are always in perfect order, their things kept tidy. Nothing on the carpet, no clothes, papers—nothing whatsoever. And the bathroom should be immaculate at all times, right children?" she asked the kids to make sure they were paying attention. I was itching for this part of the morning to end.

Chris looked rather miserable as Mrs. Brown walked over to his bed. She turned down the covers to display what looked like a straight jacket, folded neatly on top of the bottom sheet. "This is Christopher's 'sleep-safe.' He must be pinned into it at night when you tuck him in." Christopher picked at his nail. "Stop that, Christopher," said Mrs. Brown reflexively.

"Show her Mommy's room," Christina whispered. I smiled at her; the Crawford bedroom was certainly on the top of my list of Things To See and Report Back On. But it had to wait.

"Your mother is resting," Mrs. Brown answered curtly. "I'll take Missy in later." She turned to me. "Follow me downstairs, please?" We all trouped after her, out the back door to the swimming pool.

"The children swim daily. Christopher and Christina are to be timed while doing laps. The twins must practice being water safe. Miss Crawford wants you to throw them into the deep end of the pool and let them make it to the side on their own." She paused. "Any questions so far?"

Yes, I thought. *Throw them into the deep end? Are you kidding me?*

Cathy, myself, and Cindy Crawford, 1949

"No," I said, "no questions." Mrs. Brown turned back to the house. A moment later I sensed someone coming up behind me. Christopher slipped his hand into mine, and we stood a moment, watching the turquoise water shimmering in the sunlight. The day was hot, so I suggested we go in and get something to drink. Christopher stood outside the kitchen as I looked around for a couple of glasses. I was met head-on by Marie, the redhead I'd spotted on arrival. Her eyes were flashing.

"What are you doing in my kitchen?"

"I was just getting Christopher a drink."

"Next time you need something you ring for Henry. No one else comes into my kitchen!" She handed Christopher a glass of ice water and shooed us away. I certainly wasn't making friends with the staff.

When Miss Crawford went out later that day, Christina insisted I see her mother's bedroom. Mrs. Brown gave in to the request, but her expression made clear she saw me as an intruder. "Come *on,*" said Christina, pulling at me. We went in. Crawford's room could have been straight off a set—elegant and lush, all in white, down to a crystal vase of white, long-stem roses. The white satin oversized bed loaded with pillows was on the sleeping porch overlooking the garden. There were silver-framed portraits on the night table and bureau, glamour shots of Joan from various films. One could get lost in her three walk-in wardrobe closets. I counted the endless racks of shoes—five pair of each style, mostly ankle straps in different colors.

I peeked into the marbled, mirrored bathroom. Christina pointed to lacquer trays of facial creams, bars of French soap, white monogrammed terry robes, and luxurious, white monogrammed towels neatly folded on a heated stand. Mrs. Brown reached over and quickly closed the bathroom door.

"Of course, this area is off-limits at all times, unless Miss Crawford calls for you," Mrs. Brown said.

"Of course," I said. Mrs. Brown was wearing on me. "It's time for Christopher's piano lesson," I told her, heading for the stairs and taking Christina along.

"How nice you're musical," she replied. It was the only personal statement she'd made to me all day.

Christopher had his little Mozart piece down and was ready to move on to something else.

"Ever try this?" I asked him, playing the bass beat of a boogie-woogie.

Christopher giggled. "Where'd you learn that?"

"We can do it together. I'll teach you. Let me show you what the right hand does."

Christopher picked up on it almost immediately. I backed him up, and soon he was adding little riffs of his own. We were really swinging when suddenly he stopped playing all together.

"Christopher? What's the matter?"

He looked away from me. "Missy, are you going to stay?"

"I hadn't planned on leaving. I just got here. Why?"

"The nannies never stay."

"Well, maybe I'm different." I put an arm around his shoulder. He hesitated, then leaned in toward me.

Miss Crawford left for New York the next day, off to shoot *The Damned Don't Cry*.

I stood at the front door and watched the children hug her good-bye, promising to be good, while Henry hoisted a dozen Vuitton bags into the back of the studio car carrying her to the airport. "I expect you to keep everything in order," Miss Crawford called back to me briskly as the limo pulled away.

A sense of peace settled over the house as soon as she was gone. The kids were more relaxed, and Marie and Henry began to let their guard down around me, inviting me into the kitchen for some juicy gossip.

But at dinner the more casual atmosphere dissolved completely. Crawford had her children so well trained that even in her absence one would have thought they were dining with the queen. We five were seated at the round dinner table—Christopher, Christina, the twins in their high chairs, and I, self-conscious at every move. Dinner was a formal affair, with Henry serving from silver platters and Lenox china. I cut up Cindy's and Cathy's food to go on their suction plates, but the older children had been trained to use their cutlery European style—forks in their right hand, knives in their left. I felt embarrassed handling my knife and fork differently. They sat up straight, cut their food carefully, and chewed with their mouths closed. It was all very somber.

I longed for a burger, a beer, and a laugh.

6

Behind the Scenes: The Real Joan Crawford

One afternoon I was keeping Marie company in the kitchen as she prepared one of her beautiful dinners for the children and me.

"Everything you make is a feast for the eyes," I told her, watching her carefully layer lemon slices over chicken that had been marinated in white wine and thyme. "And so delicious." I nibbled on one of the miniature chocolate pecan cookies she'd baked that morning. "My friends are jealous when I tell them I'm on a gourmet diet."

"Invite them over," Marie said.

"Excuse me?"

"Have a party. Who's going to know? Miss C. isn't back for another two weeks. You could ask anyone you like. Ask that boyfriend you supposedly don't have anymore."

"As a matter of fact, he's back in town."

"Good. We'll have a real shindig. I'll make whatever you want. I'd like cooking for your friends."

"Oh, Marie!" Impulsively I reached down and hugged her. She didn't exactly hug me back; it was more like a tentative series of pats on my shoulder.

"For God's sake," she said, going back to her cutting board. "It's only food!"

But with Marie it was never only food. She took so much pride in everything that came out of her kitchen that I knew when she said "a real shindig," she meant to break out the best.

"Stuffed mushrooms?" Marie asked me suddenly the next day. "No. Boring. Wild mushroom tarts and stuffed shrimp." She had started writing a detailed menu for my party. "I need a guest list by tomorrow," she added, chewing on a pencil.

The guest list was a challenge. Joanne and Bev were the obvious first guests, and then my friend Robert Walker and my on-and-off again boyfriend, Bob, who was visiting from New York. I decided to invite Roger Edens and Jerry. Roger had known Crawford at MGM, before she was let go. I was sure his presence would bring amusing stories.

More troubling was whether or not I would invite my father and Faye. I could picture Daddy walking up the long path to the mansion's front door. Faye would be there, in the highest of high heels, tottering beside him, her lip-sticked mouth open in awe at where I had landed. Daddy would be giving her a nudge in the ribs, as if to say, "Look at this, huh? My little girl living with a movie star!" There was no doubt about it. I'd finally impress him. It would be so much fun to see them sitting in the Crawford living room, Daddy sipping a martini, Faye with her usual Coke. I could imagine telling them stories about Crawford that would actually make my job seem funny. They'd be excited by how far I'd come.

"Great to hear from you!" Daddy boomed when I rang him the next day. "When do I get to see my little girl? Still so busy?"

"No, no, everything's great. I'll tell you all about it when I come to visit you tomorrow. It's my day off."

The next afternoon I called upstairs, "I'm home," as I came in the front door. There was no answer. "Daddy?"

Nothing. Maybe he and Faye had stepped out for a minute. I went into the kitchen to get a snack, saw the stale cold cuts in the refrigerator, and changed my mind. Suddenly I heard a scratching sound coming from inside the pantry door, followed by what sounded like a high whine. *What on earth?* I opened the pantry door and jumped back as Daddy's little Chow, Oscar, scrambled out and ran past me up the stairs. I followed him but stopped in my tracks when I got to the door of the master bedroom. Daddy, in his underwear, and Faye, in panties and bra, were tied to the bedposts. There was masking tape over their mouths. Oscar licked Daddy's red face as I untied them. Faye immediately dashed into the bathroom. Mumbling, my father ripped off the tape.

"Fuckin' gorillas," he sneered. He got up and raced to the open wall safe. It was empty. "Shit!" he yelled. "They didn't have to take my lucky dice!" He rushed to the phone and dialed. His voice was full of contempt. "What was the hurry? You couldn't wait one more day? You know my word's good . . . You cleaned me out . . . Yeah, yeah, I know. Better tell your fuckin' henchmen they don't know who they're messin' with." After a long pause my father hung up. "We have to be out of here in a week," he announced solemnly. He had bet the house in a poker game and had lost.

He was in better spirits a few hours later—cleaned up and drinking a scotch as Faye was starting to wrap their china in newspaper.

"Where will you go, Daddy?"

"I've still got a few tricks up my sleeve, kiddo. Tell me about this soiree you're having tomorrow. We'd love to come, right, Faye?"

"Of course we'll be there, honey."

I had purposefully arranged for a late get-together so I'd have time to feed the kids and get them into bed before anyone arrived. There wasn't any other live-in staff, so I almost relaxed as Marie laid out exquisite appetizers and Henry made sure we had a full bar.

My boyfriend, Bob, arrived first, and we slipped upstairs to be alone for a minute. "Miss you," he murmured between kisses. "When are you going to be ready to move to New York?"

"When are you going to come back home?" I teased. We'd had this conversation so many times it didn't mean much anymore.

The doorbell rang. I could tell as soon as I saw Daddy that he'd already had a few. "Some digs!" he exclaimed, staring up at the high ceilings and then at the long, winding staircase as soon as he and Faye had stepped inside. I winced, thinking of what the scene must be in their home, with packing boxes everywhere. But he seemed cheerful and animated. "I can't believe my little girl is living with the great Joan Crawford. I guess by now you're practically one of the family."

"Well, not really, Daddy. She doesn't exactly mingle with the help."

"It takes a while. I look forward to meeting her sometime."

That'll be the day, I thought. I excused myself to answer the door, glad that the company had arrived before Daddy could ask for a tour.

"Come on, everyone, let's have a drink," I said, leading them to the bar.

The buffet table was set for a feast. With Henry pouring and Marie passing trays of her hors d'ouvres, it was easy to settle in. "Great liverwurst," Robert said as he took a huge chunk of pate from a platter. Marie had told me the pâté cost $100 an ounce.

The party was going so well that, many drinks later, when Faye begged to be shown the upstairs, I said, "Sure!" and led the way. Daddy and Faye brought up the rear; she actually snapped photographs as if she were on some fans' tour. I didn't want to risk waking the kids, so I directed everyone with a whisper down the hall into the master suite, the most intriguing room to see.

This was my party, but we were all very aware that it was Joan Crawford's house. Joanne was more at home than any of the rest of us, as she'd seen all this kind of thing before and wasn't impressed. In fact, when I turned around, she was gone.

"Joanne," I said quietly, "whatever you're doing, stop it."

"Joanne? That's *Joan* to you," said a voice from within one of the walk-in closets. Then out she came bedecked in classic Crawford: a Chanel suit with shoulder pads, a Rex hat, and ankle strap shoes. She'd even slashed some blood red lipstick over her mouth. She grabbed Crawford's Oscar.

"Thank you, thank you, my darlings, for this wonderful honor!" she cried.

"Would you please—" I laughed, my sentence interrupted by Bob throwing me onto Crawford's enormous, plush bed. That did it.

"This party's getting out of hand," I said as I crawled out of the pillows. "Time to call it a night."

But it had been fun, if more than vaguely surreal.

On his way out my father picked up a photograph of Crawford standing in front of a '49 Cadillac. "Tell Joan if she needs a new Caddy to call your daddy."

My next day off I spent helping Faye and Daddy pack for the movers. Late in the afternoon he and I sat in the patio watching the last of the garden furniture being carted into the moving van. A hefty guy came over to where we were seated, excused himself, and carried off the umbrella and table. In a few minutes he came back, and we stood so he could take our chairs.

"I'm sorry you have to move out of your beautiful home," I said.

He looked around at his surroundings and shrugged. "It's just a house. Don't worry about it. It's okay. I rented a little apartment over near Vermont Avenue, so we have a roof over our heads. And before you know it I'll move into another house. Bigger and better, you'll see." His spirits began to lift. "Those who play must pay, kiddo. Your daddy's not beaten.

Not by a long shot. Always remember: anyone can play a good hand. It's how you play a bad hand that counts." By the time I said good-bye, he sounded ready to buy Las Vegas.

Crawford called several times while she was away to speak to the kids, but other than that we had no contact. When Marie mentioned that the boss was on her way home from New York, I felt more curious than anything else. Joanne had filled me in on Crawford's career, which apparently was taking a dive. I'd thought of her as Hollywood royalty, having read about her Oscar win for *Mildred Pierce*. Academy Awards were not shown on television yet, but they still received big press. Joanne said Crawford had been dropped by MGM, that *Pierce* was a fluke, and she had been left stuck with pulp films, B movies. Joanne added that on the set she could be a bitch on wheels. "Stay out of her way when she gets back," she advised me.

Miss Crawford arrived home Saturday night, looking tired but clearly pleased to see the children well behaved and beautifully dressed. She kissed each one and within five minutes was upstairs to bed.

Late the next morning the kids and I were working on math problems in the garden before lunch. I'd made up some game that had us multiplying elephants and kangaroos, and the kids were laughing, quite loudly. Their mother suddenly appeared on the balcony of her bedroom, bleary-eyed but unmistakably in a snit.

"What the hell is going on down here?" she hissed at me. I felt my toes turn inward.

"You've got to be kidding me!" she snapped. "Is this what I pay you for?" Before I could say anything, she was onto the kids.

"You *woke me up*."

God forbid, I thought. *It's almost noon.*

"Go to your rooms and stay there until dinner." She turned on her heel and slammed the door. My shoulders dropped. The kids looked miserable.

"We better go upstairs," I whispered to them. "Don't worry. I'll bring up some sandwiches."

As the weeks passed, it became clear that Crawford's temper ruled Christopher and Christina. With the twins, for some reason, it was different. They seemed to escape her fury, maybe because they were so young. But the two older ones were wound into knots from living under the threat of the next angry outburst over some minor mistake. Walking on glass, they often spoke only a few quiet words, or none at all, a means of getting through a childhood that was sadly familiar to me.

*   *   *

I was four. The only place I felt safe was in my mother's bed at Grandma and Grandpa Rundquist's house in Sedro-Woolley. I was born in that bed. My mother had left my father to come home for my birth and never went back to him.

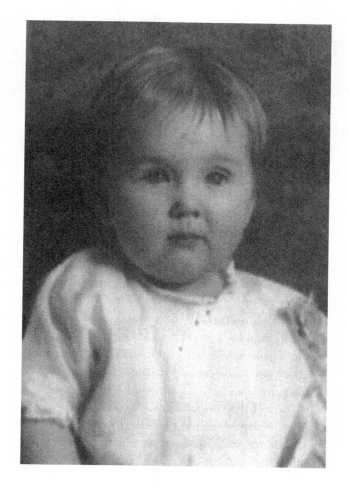

Baby Betty

A couple of years later she married her high school sweetheart, Elburn, known as "Fat" because of his size—and moved out, leaving my older brother, Dickey, and me behind to live with her parents. We rarely saw her.

My childhood home in Sedro-Woolley, Washington

My grandpa, a cabinetmaker, had built their house by himself. My favorite room in the house was the yellow kitchen, where Grandma oiled the wooden counters to a soft sheen. She kept flour, sugar, bread, and cookies in tin-lined drawers, and there was a cool-air pantry for eggs, cheese, fruit, and vegetables. I loved the kitchen so much not only because Grandma would let me help her, in little ways, but she actually spoke to me as we prepared meals together. For the rest of the day, Dickey and I had only each other to talk to. Growing up in a house of silence, we weren't exactly the most boisterous or playful children.

After meals, Grandma washed the dishes while I dried. She would sweep the kitchen floor, and then we sat quietly by the window in the dining room, she in her rocking chair and I in the smaller rocker Grandpa had made for me. Grandpa and Grandma were very good to each other, but, as is customary in the Scandinavian culture, they showed little affection and there was little conversation. In their presence my brother and I learned to be seen and not heard.

* * *

Despite the incessant tension between Crawford, Christopher, and Christina, she was completely obsessed with her public image of the "perfect mother," and many professional photos were taken with "Mommy." Those famous matching outfits she and Christina would wear had their own closet, and I was responsible for making sure they were kept starched and pressed, every bow and frill in place. They looked like what they were: costumes.

Hollywood actresses showing off their children was big press, and when the *L.A. Times* announced its "Mother of the Year" event, timed to coincide with Mother's Day, Crawford hinted to me more than once that she felt she stood a good chance of winning. She was furious when she lost out to Dinah Shore.

"She's a singer, for God's sake. And not a very good one at that!" Crawford fumed, throwing the paper down on the breakfast table. Later that day she came to me and told me to write a congratulatory note to Miss Shore. Then she dictated a guest list for invitations to Christina's upcoming eleventh birthday party.

Every birthday was an extravaganza, with celebrities and their children—and, of course, always the press—in attendance. Christina's party was a circus, literally. There were clowns and a carousel and ponies decorated with plumes for the children to ride. Christina was photographed surrounded by dozens and dozens of gifts. I winced at the sight of them, knowing these extravagantly wrapped presents would soon be delegated to the "gift closet" to be given away to other, "more deserving," children.

On July 16, 1949, even I received a few recycled presents from that closet. Miss Crawford arranged a surprise twenty-first birthday party for me, with gifts of soap, cologne, and a book of her publicity shots.

"Now, blow out the candles and make a wish," Crawford said. There was one of Marie's large, frosted, chocolate mousse cakes with roses on the icing and "Happy Birthday Missy" written in the center.

"Every birthday is special," Miss Crawford announced after I thanked her for her generosity. The kids and staff had caught this performance many times before, but I couldn't help being taken in by all the attention, even though it felt strange. In my entire life, I had only had one other birthday party.

Marie caught me on the way to the gift closet later in the day. She lifted a simple but chic cotton skirt from the top of the basket.

"Isn't this your size? It's perfect for you."

"I can't take Miss Crawford's things!" I laughed.

"It's all going to charity anyway," Marie shrugged. "She wouldn't care. Probably not even notice."

A few days later, however, my boss spotted me wearing the skirt and stopped me in the hall. "Miss Ebeling," she said. She always called me by my last name, rather than "Missy," when she wanted to pull rank. "Where did you get that skirt?"

I recognized that voice, having heard it directed toward her own children.

"It was in the donation basket . . ." I faltered.

"And who gave you permission to take it from the basket?"

"I was told they were clothes to be given away. I thought it would be all right."

"Well, you thought wrong. I will not have anyone in my house who steals."

I had never stolen anything in my life. Not even candy as a kid. "I'm sorry. I didn't know."

"If I catch you taking anything again, you'll be fired."

"I understand." I stood there motionless as she turned and walked away.

That night I wanted to call Joanne and turn the story into a funny anecdote—Crawford acting with me as though the cameras were rolling—but the experience still left me on edge. I put it on the list of things to tell my friends later, although I was seeing less and less of them. Joanne was moving home to New York and even though we promised to stay in touch, eventually we drifted apart.

My boyfriend Bob was returning to New York, so we made plans for a date the night before he left. I made clear to Miss Crawford, in the firmest tone I could summon, that I would be out that night.

Bob and I went to a romantic Hungarian restaurant. Violins serenaded us over goulash. "I'll miss you," I said. We'd had rather a lot to drink, and when a fortune-teller came to our table, we invited her to join us. She read my future: "You will be married before the year is over." Bob and I gave each other a kiss. "But not to this man." We were taken aback, but when she left the table, Bob laughed and was soon kissing my neck. "How about I come home with you this evening so we both have something to remember until I'm back?"

"You know Crawford's rules," I said. We reluctantly said good-bye with a long kiss but nothing more.

As I was undressing for bed I heard pebbles on my upstairs window. I stood on my tiny balcony to see Bob clumsily climbing up the trellis to my room. Marie peered out her window and called softly, "How romantic."

Bob was blowing smoke rings as we lay in each other's arms after making love. That should have been the moment I kissed him, handed him his clothes, and hurried him out the way he'd come in. Instead, we drifted off to sleep. I was awakened by a frantic whisper and knocking on my door.

"Missy?" It was Miss Crawford.

"Yes?" I answered in a state of panic. Bob lay stock-still, not breathing.

"Could you please help me? Someone has broken in. I think he's hiding downstairs." She couldn't have heard Bob from her room, could she? His covert entrance must have made just enough noise to enter her dreams.

"I'm coming," I called out to her, nodding at the window to Bob as I put on my robe. I slipped out of the room, and Miss Crawford took my hand as I led the tour of the house, checking all seventy-two closets.

"There's no one here," I reassured her. She held onto me as if someone was about to spring out at us any moment.

"You had a bad dream," I told her. She looked like a little girl at that moment, vulnerable and frightened. I walked her to her bedroom and watched as she climbed back into bed. It was good the whole incident took as much time as it did; every trace of Robert was gone by the time I got back to my room.

The next evening I discovered I wasn't the only one who had clandestine visitors; there was a terrible commotion outside my bedroom window, and I went to see what on earth could be going on. There I saw the butler, Henry, and the night security guard having sex in the bushes. I stared for a minute, shocked by the sight, then went back to bed. The next morning I told Marie what I had seen.

"Oh, Henry," she chuckled. "He can't help himself. Probably the only fun the poor guy has." Henry was the perfect, passive, stoic butler. Except in the bushes.

Marie was easily the most empathetic of everyone living under Crawford's roof. I remember once passing through the kitchen and spying a stack of garishly wrapped presents on top of a china closet.

"Santa come early, Marie?"

"Nope," said Marie, chopping vegetables. "They're from Anna, gifts for the children." Anna was Crawford's mother, who I'd never seen; she was essentially banned from the house. Marie reached for the gifts. "I better put them away before anyone else sees them. I try to give the kids things their grandma drops off, but if their mother finds out, she'll just toss 'em."

Crawford decided on impulse to give herself one of her famous parties. She put me to work on the invitations. I couldn't help noticing every guest happened to be male. Most of her parties were like that—filled with handsome men who doted on Crawford but flirted mostly with each other.

The party put Marie back to work creating one of her peerless menus. She had contacts everywhere and could easily command lobsters flown in from Maine, smoked salmon from Scotland, and prime cuts of beef from a ranch in Texas. She picked herbs and vegetables from her own kitchen garden. She gathered and sugar-powdered roses to lie next to the chocolate mousse. I did my best to keep out of her kitchen, but the night of the party I couldn't resist watching her lay on the finishing touches.

Long before the guests arrived, the children were to be upstairs and completely quiet. I slipped down the back stairs to take a peek and spied more than a dozen men in black tie seated in the formal dining room. Marie, in her white, starched uniform, was relaxing at the small service table, sipping coffee laced with brandy, puffing on a cigarette, and giving orders to Henry. She never rushed. In fact, she barely moved.

Later Henry called me on the house phone. "Miss Crawford wants the children down in fifteen minutes, Missy."

"Fifteen minutes," I told the kids, switching into stage manager mode. Poor babies. Every social gathering meant a demand performance from each of them. I lined them up, inspecting each child carefully to make sure their bathrobes were properly tied over their very best PJs and every hair was perfectly in place. Christina's golden waves, especially, had to be just right. "Off we go," I whispered, leading them to the staircase.

Crawford saw us at the foot of the stairs and gave me the nod, and I brought them in. Christopher and Christina were old enough to say a quick hello just as the guests were finishing dessert, with Christopher giving a little bow. The twins stood shyly, one on either side of me, holding my hands. Dessert finished, it was show time. One by one, in order of age, Christina first, the children approached their mother. Placing one small palm on either side of her face, each child in turn planted a kiss with every word: "I," kiss the left eye; "Love," kiss the right eye; "You," kiss right on the tip of her nose; "Mommy," quick kiss on the chin; and finally "Dearest," a kiss on the mouth. At the table, the men were all smiles. Wasn't this too adorable?

"Now off you go, my darlings," Crawford said with a wide-eyed, gleaming smile. I never knew where to look when she put on that face. It was as if she was frozen in close-up. I just gently turned to the kids and, true to form, they followed me in procession out of the room.

After I got the kids to bed, Christopher strapped in, uncomplaining as always, Christina asking to stay up and read. I went downstairs to see if Henry or Marie needed me. Crawford had set up a screening of *Mildred Pierce* in the projection room. I helped Henry bring in a tray of cognac, port, and crystal snifters just as the film began. As Henry poured with his usual heavy hand, Crawford whispered to me, "You can stay, Missy," and even patted a chair next to her. I sat, feeling terribly self-conscious.

But the film pulled me in and I forgot my surroundings until Miss Crawford, on her third cognac, signaled the projectionist to rerun the previous scene. "Do you realize I did that whole scene in one take? I set a record." She paused. Someone was softly snoring. Miss Crawford got up and walked over to an older gentleman, fast asleep in a large wing chair, and kicked him in the shin, hard. He woke with a start. "Walter, if you need your rest, I'll excuse you." The fellow made an embarrassed apology and headed for the door. I wished I could have followed him but the film resumed immediately, and with the star by my side, it was clear I wasn't going anywhere.

A few more scenes in, Miss Crawford herself got up and slipped out, going up to her bedroom. From there she telephoned me on the staff phone. "Get rid of them," she ordered quietly. Awkwardly, I told the guests their hostess was terribly sorry, but she had a headache and the party was over, even though the film hadn't ended. They smirked and nodded knowingly.

Later that night I had trouble sleeping. I went downstairs in my pajamas to get a cup of tea, but before I stepped into the kitchen, I could hear someone was already there. I looked in, unseen, to find Miss Crawford, still in her Christian Dior gown, on her hands and knees scrubbing the floor. By now she was very drunk, mumbling, "Look at me . . . I don't need this shit. I spend a fucking fortune and for what? This place is a mess. I'm firing Marie. I'm firing Henry. I'm firing everybody, including that new nanny, whatever the fuck her name is."

The next morning she called me into her dressing room to find her hangover prescription, obviously having no recollection of her threats from the night before.

Protecting the children from this crazy lady became my mission in life. As time went on, they began to rebel and things went from bad to worse. One evening at the dinner table when Christina refused to eat okra, her mother turned on her with a look of pure hatred and said in a slow, icy, voice, "If you dare disobey me, I will take you back where I found you and show you where you really belong."

In spite of the children's protests I resigned twice, only to be cajoled into returning when Miss Crawford went on location. When I finally left for good, she was furious. "I'll never forgive you for this, you selfish, ungrateful bitch," were her parting words. Perfectly delivered.

Right out of a movie.

Shortly after I left the Crawford home, Bette Davis called me.

"I've heard wonderful things about you," she began, telling me she was looking for a nanny for her children.

"No, thank you," I replied. Never again.

7

Hold Onto Your Seats for a Whirlwind Romance

My home after leaving Crawford's was a far cry from her Brentwood estate. Joanne and Bev were both living in New York, so I rented a small studio apartment above a garage, off an alley in Beverly Hills, and took a secretarial job at a store called Rattancraft. It paid the bills, with enough money left over to continue my vocal training with Erv from UCLA and free time to work with Roger. That's what mattered.

Robert Walker and I stayed in touch after I left Crawford's, and it was inadvertently again because of him that my life took another unexpected turn.

One rainy Saturday he called to take me to a party on the Sunset Strip being given by some new starlet his agency had taken on. Beverly, working in the theater, was visiting from New York, and Robert said he would take us both. The party was packed, full of young actors and other film industry hopefuls. I went into the kitchen to get something to drink and noticed a tall, lean, rather intense man in his midtwenties doing tricks with a yo-yo. We did not speak.

As the evening progressed, I found myself trapped between two boring actors, both vying for attention. Bev was across the room flirting with an attractive young man. I wanted to leave, but Robert was nowhere to be seen. He probably had met a new cute actor in town and took him out for drinks, ostensibly for business purposes. The rain was coming down in buckets, and I had no money for a cab. The man with the yo-yo passed by, and I turned to him.

Lee and I meet

"Excuse me, but do you have a car?"

"I do," he said. I liked the sound of his deep, resonant voice.

"I live only ten minutes away, and my escort seems to have left me. Could you drive me home?"

His eyes twinkled and his full lips parted in a half-smile. "Poor baby. It would be a privilege," he said. *Quite the charmer,* I thought.

I grabbed Beverly. "Robert left us. We have a ride. Let's go."

"What's your name?" our driver asked as we got into his 1948 black Ford convertible.

"Betty Ebeling. And yours?" I was trying to be friendly.

"Lee Marvin."

"I suppose you're an actor too," I said sarcastically.

"Isn't everyone?" he chuckled.

When we pulled up in the alley, I just wanted to jump out, say my thanks, and get out of the rain. I was waiting for a phone call from my boyfriend Bob in New York. I'd been thinking of him all night.

There was no phone call that night, but the next morning, finally, the phone rang. It had to be my Bob.

"Good morning, darling," I said, trying to sound cheerful.

"Same to you, sweetheart."

I recognized Lee's deep voice. "Oh, sorry."

"Don't be. I'm not." What a flirt.

"How'd you get my number?"

"I have my ways. I just came in from fly fishing in the park and thought I'd take you to lunch."

"Fly-fishing in the park?"

"Yeah. On the lawn."

"Catch anything?"

He laughed. "I miss Montauk Point."

"Sorry about lunch. I'm going with a friend to hear jazz at the Lighthouse in Manhattan Beach."

"What about dinner?"

"I have a dinner date."

"How about after dinner?" he persisted. I started to laugh.

"Look, I'm practically engaged. My boyfriend is in New York, and I don't think he would appreciate my going out with you."

He was undaunted. "So? I have a girlfriend in Manhattan. What's wrong with our keeping each other company? I don't know many people out here . . . I'm lonely. I like you."

"Sorry, I have to go. I'm expecting an important call. Besides, I think you could be trouble." He laughed. I hung up.

The phone rang. It was Lee.

"Just want you to know I don't give up easily."

Bob never called.

When I came home from dinner that night, I was surprised to see Lee's car parked in the alley. He was sitting on the steps leading up to my studio.

"I don't believe this," I said.

"Hi," he said casually. "Coffee?"

"Okay. Coffee. But that's all."

He took my hand as we sped toward the beach with the top down. "You know, I could fall madly in love with you."

"You don't even know me."

"My agent wants me to stay in Hollywood and work as a character actor in films. Let's live together at the beach."

"We're not living together anywhere. We're just going out for a cup of coffee. I'm engaged, remember?"

"You don't want to marry that guy."

"Yes I do."

Lee pulled over to the curb. He took my hand and looked at the ring on my wedding finger. Though it was more of a promise of an engagement ring, it seemed wise not to mention that at the moment. Then, before I could so much as blink, Lee's long fingers were twisted around mine.

"Let's get rid of that thing." He quickly slipped off the ring, put it into his pocket, and continued driving up the coast.

"You've got one hell of a nerve. Who do you think you are?"

"The man who adores you."

"Oh, please. You're nuts. Pull over. Give me back my ring and let me out of this car."

Lee stopped the car and took me in his arms. I tried to push him away. "What are you doing? Stop this," I pleaded halfheartedly.

He kissed me gently, then cupped my face in his hands and kissed me again. "You'll grow to love me," he whispered.

The next morning, Sunday, Lee called—and called and called. I tried to plead off, but he was adamant. It wasn't that I didn't want to see him, but his intensity made me wary. Isn't a guy supposed to wait a day or two? After the first two calls, I stopped answering the phone. I went out for a walk and even thought of stopping by work, although I wasn't expected until Monday.

When I came back into the apartment, the phone was ringing. I gave in.

"Hello?"

"Let's have brunch. There's a place I want to take you to."

"I don't think—"

"I'll be over in an hour. We're gonna have a wild day."

"Okay, okay!" At that point we were both laughing.

"See you," Lee said and hung up before I could change my mind.

We drove through bright morning sunlight, the radio turned up, playing vintage blues.

"The only music worth listening to," said Lee, lending his deep bass to Leadbelly's twelve-string guitar.

"So where is this place?"

"Almost there," he said, making a sharp turn. I looked, and next thing I knew we were headed toward the Santa Monica Pier Amusement Park.

"I thought we were going out to brunch."

"We are. Just wanted to show you something first."

Opening the door for me, Lee took my hand and guided me immediately toward the nearest shooting gallery. He put down his money, picked up the gallery's rifle, and hit every sitting duck—*bing, bing, bing.* The young kid behind the stand stood there open-mouthed.

"Guess you can choose whatever you want, Mister," he said, pointing to the shelves of prizes behind him.

Lee chose a huge monkey. "Give it to the lady."

I felt a little silly walking into the café on the Santa Monica pier holding the oversized stuffed animal, but Lee insisted he be our escort and sat him in a chair at our table.

After that Lee and I rarely spent a day apart. Ours was a whirlwind courtship with intimate dinners in the best restaurants, long drives up and down the coast, and romantic nights at beach hideaways. I began having trouble remembering what had been so important in my life before we met, and my dreams of a career seemed to be fading.

One evening, a few weeks into the love affair, I was rehearsing with Roger in his music studio. I looked up and saw Lee sitting in the open French window watching me perform. I stopped in the middle of my song. He applauded. Roger looked up in surprise.

"What are you doing here?" I said.

"Watching you," Lee said. He jumped down, came over and introduced himself to Roger.

Later that evening we were together in my little apartment. "I hope you don't take your singing and dancing with Mr. MGM seriously," Lee said. "There'll be only one career in this family."

I tried not to hear that. My singing lessons were my life's blood. Could I so easily give up all plans for a career after years of training?

8

Love and Marriage Is Every Girl's Goal

Three months later I was madly in love and pregnant. It's not what I had in mind for myself at the time, but we all know life is what happens while we're making other plans—and life had definitely happened inside me. The thought of an abortion never entered my mind, even though I was frightened and overwhelmed by the thought of having to grow up in nine months and be responsible for a baby. I certainly couldn't turn to my mother for guidance.

I knew I had to tell Lee but had no idea how he'd react. We were deeply in love, but he was a free spirit with big plans for a career. When I summoned up my courage and told him I was pregnant, he said little, but once in bed, it didn't seem to matter. Still, the next day I found myself wondering where this was going and how I would manage if I had to raise a child on my own.

Two nights later we celebrated April Fool's Day at one of our favorite restaurants, the famous Cock N Bull on Sunset Strip. After his two martinis and my Dubonnet and soda—the only drink I could tolerate during pregnancy—I ordered Welsh rarebit and he asked for the beefsteak and kidney pie with a bottle of their best cabernet. After dinner Lee pulled me to him.

"Betty, you are the only woman I've ever loved."

"Oh, sure, April Fool, right?"

"I'm serious. I can't do better. I want to marry you."

I fell silent, wondering if he was proposing because he felt he had to. He must have read my mind.

"This isn't a shotgun proposal," he said. "I love you. I want to spend the rest of my life with you. What do you say?"

I happily said yes.

We rented a small, one-bedroom, furnished apartment in Beverly Hills and brought our few personal possessions there to set up housekeeping. We decided to marry as soon as possible and not tell our family or friends about the pregnancy. As if they couldn't count. Because we were both working, we planned to drive to Las Vegas early Saturday morning, be married that evening, and return on Sunday. I bought a pink, silk, sleeveless shell, street-length dress with a brocade bodice. I didn't think white would be appropriate in my condition. I also bought a sexy, ice-blue, satin nightgown that I could ill afford and never wore. Lee packed a white shirt and tie and threw a sports jacket in the trunk, and we were off. We drove most of the day through the hot desert with the top down. My face and arms were sunburned and my long, blond hair was like straw by the time we saw the lights of Las Vegas. We stopped at a Chevron station on the outskirts of town and went into separate restrooms to change. I splashed water on my face, put on a little makeup, and, in that tiny gas station bathroom, struggled into my wedding dress. When I inched outside, clutching my bag of cast-off clothes, Lee was leaning against the wall, waiting for me.

"You look beautiful," he said.

Setting off to find a chapel—no problem in a place where all gambling is fast and easy—we soon came upon a Queen Anne Victorian house on the strip with a neon sign brightly announcing "Wee Kirk of the Heather. Weddings performed here. No reservations required." It seemed the perfect choice.

Arriving at the top of the stairs we hesitated, then turned to each other. Lee put his arms around me. "This feels right," he said and gave me a quick kiss. When we rang the doorbell, wedding chimes sounded, the door opened, and we were greeted by a short, round, middle-aged man with a jolly face who, if one added a beard, could have substituted for Santa.

"Come on in, lovebirds. I'm Reverend Loveable," he said. With a flip of a switch, organ music played in the background and electric candles glowed on an altar that was adorned with artificial white roses. I was about to laugh, but Lee restrained me by squeezing my right hand.

"Have you got a witness?" the Reverend Loveable asked cheerfully. We shook our heads. "That's okay. I'll get my wife." He left the room and returned shortly with a plain-looking woman in an Indian flannel bathrobe and beaded moccasins. She remained silent and detached, partially hidden behind a screen in the corner of the room.

"One more thing," Loveable said. He left the room again, returning with a bunch of artificial lilies of the valley for me to hold.

"Thank you," I said, biting my lip.

"Now, do you want the long or short version?" asked Loveable.

"What's the difference?" Lee asked.

"Well, the cheap one just covers the basics, takes five minutes, and costs twenty-five dollars. I recommend the one with some words from the Bible, fifteen minutes for forty bucks."

"What the hell," Lee said. "Give us the full treatment." We took our places and the Reverend Loveable began to ramble on about marriage being like a rose garden and the importance of pulling out the weeds as we walked along the path. He then recited the Lord's Prayer. I thought this a strange choice for a wedding, particularly the "forgive us our trespasses" part. After we promised to love and obey, Lee put a gold band on my finger, Loveable pronounced us man and wife, and we kissed. Our time was up.

When Lee took out his wallet to pay for the service, the Reverend Loveable offered to sell us a record of the ceremony for a small additional fee. We declined, a decision I always regretted.

We had no reservation and there were no rooms available in the Sahara or either of the other two hotels, so we spent our wedding night with Lee drinking a bottle of champagne while he rolled craps in the Sahara casino. Then we began the long drive back to Los Angeles. "This place is in the middle of nowhere," I said, snuggling next to my husband and leaving the lights behind.

"And not enough beds," Lee said. "A guy gets married and can't even get laid."

On our way out of town we passed a Marine hitchhiking. Lee slammed on the brakes. "Can't leave a fellow Marine in the desert." The young man was drunk and soon passed out on my shoulder. Lee glanced over as I was drifting off. "I don't believe it!" he said. "My bride ends up sleeping with a drunk Marine on our wedding night, and it wasn't even me!"

We spent our Sunday honeymoon in bed. That afternoon, on his second bottle of champagne, Lee spontaneously picked up the phone and called his family.

"Congratulate me! I just called to tell you I'm a married man and you're going to be grandparents!"

It was a short conversation. No one asked to speak to me. Lee hung up, made light of it, and filled his glass.

"Now it's your turn. Better call your mom."

"Do I have to?"

"Come on, sweetheart. You should tell her."

"Why? She has no interest in what I'm doing. I could be a hooker for all she knows."

Lee laughed. "Well, let her know I've made an honest woman of you."

He wouldn't let it go, so I finally gave in and called my mother. "That's nice," she said when I gave her the news. She seemed impressed when I told her my husband was an actor and wanted to know if she could see him in the movies or on TV. "I look forward to meeting my new son-in-law and grandchild," she said before we hung up. She never asked how I was. I was surprised she didn't ask who I was.

Lee and I happily married

The next morning, heading out the door for the studio, Lee called back, "I hope you can cook, sweetheart. We can't live on love alone, and I'm sick of eating out."

"Don't worry about it," I said, blowing him a kiss. "Bye, love."

Lee walked out the door. I ran to the kitchen. *Oh, boy, I'm screwed*, I thought. My cooking skills ended with boiling water. I needed an expert. I called Crawford's home, knowing Marie had been taken back after Crawford fired her.

"Hello?" A young woman answered the phone. *Poor thing*, I thought. *You must be my replacement.*

"Hello, may I please speak with Marie?"

"Who shall I say is calling?"

I started to give my name and then stopped, imagining Joan Crawford standing right there in the room, like a vulture waiting to descend.

"Just an old friend."

When Marie realized who I was, she took the call privately, in the back pantry. I quickly told her my plight.

"Good God, Missy, I thought you were too smart to get married."

"I fell in love."

"What about your career?"

"My husband says one performer in the family is enough."

"What does he do?"

"He's an actor."

"Oh, brother. Didn't you get your fill of actors living here? You work your way through college, then put up with Madame to pay for voice lessons, and now you're gonna give up your dreams of a career. Why do you wanna settle down and be a cook? At least I get paid for it."

"Marie, just help me!" I pleaded, laughing.

The next day was Marie's day off from work and, as soon as Lee was gone, she showed up. She looked around our tiny apartment and raised an eyebrow.

"This closet is your kitchen?"

"I know, it's small, but—"

Marie waved me off, going through every cabinet, taking out our three pots and pans. She gave a sigh and reached into her bag for a Lucky Strike. "Let's start with money. What's your grocery budget?"

"Fifty dollars a week."

"Jesus, Betty, I spend that on dinner! But okay."

Together we made up a shopping list.

"Now here are the rules," she said, puffing away. "First, the kitchen is off-limits to all but you. All your experiments will leave a mess, and you gotta keep your mistakes hidden." That was going to be tricky since there was a swinging door between the kitchen and dining area. I contemplated putting a sliding lock on the door.

"Never open a can if fresh is available," Marie said. Homemade means 'made at home.' Bread, soup, everything, comes from scratch, promise?"

I nodded. She peered into my Frigidaire and found an apple, a head of iceberg lettuce, a loaf of Wonder bread, a stick of butter, and a dozen eggs. "Well, at least there isn't much to throw out," she said.

"What the hell is this?" she asked, reaching into the cupboard and taking out a jar of Sanka.

"It's coffee."

"Oooh, baby, we got a lotta work to do."

Marie tossed the orange-labeled container into the trash, grabbed me by the elbow, and led me out of the kitchen. It was time to shop.

She introduced me to her special butcher at the Doheny Market and told him to take good care of me. Then she bought all the necessities for my cooking lessons.

Arriving back at the apartment, Marie took off and I was left with bags of groceries. Exhaustion suddenly hit me. It was getting into late afternoon, and Lee would be home in a couple of hours. All I wanted to do was lie down. After putting a few things away, I walked out of the kitchen and sank into a living room chair. What if Marie was right? What if all of this was a mistake? Married, pregnant, trapped. Years of training, only to end up with a guy who wants me to stay home and cook. I closed my eyes.

When Lee came home, I was in the middle of the living room singing, "Happiness Is Just a Thing Called Joe." He stopped and listened for a minute, then came up and embraced me. "The name's Lee," he said and stopped my voice by placing his mouth over mine.

The groceries remained untouched in the kitchen.

Learning to cook became my mission, so for the next few weeks my daily life revolved around experiments in the kitchen followed by long phone calls with Marie.

"This can't be right! It's all lumpy!" I was stirring what I had hoped would be béchamel sauce. It looked more like pancake batter.

"More hot milk, Betty, and use the whisk." I could hear Marie smoking.

"How long before I take the lamb out of the oven?"

"It isn't out yet? Hang up and get that baby out of there before it turns to leather."

Flipping through the mail one afternoon, I spied a cream-colored envelope addressed to me from Courtenay Davidge Marvin. My hand trembled as I opened my mother-in-law's letter:

Dear Betty,

My husband and I have recently learned of your marriage to our son Lee. I must say I was quite shocked. I thought he was engaged to Helen. That boy is certainly full of surprises. I congratulate you. Lee is a wonderful catch. I'm sure we'll meet one day.

Sincerely,

Courtenay Davidge Marvin

There was no mention of the coming baby.

Before long I was managing more complex menus with perfect sauces, special desserts—things I remembered from Marie's kitchen in the Crawford home. Lee's bragging gained me the reputation of being a fine cook. He began to invite members of the cast to dinner spontaneously. I did my best to make it seem like no big deal. "But nobody comes into my kitchen!" I would always announce. Good thing nobody did. They would have found me in a total panic, trying to figure out how to turn a dinner for two into a feast for four.

Finally, I could keep up the pretense no longer and invited Marie to the apartment on her day off to prepare one of her special dinners. In the middle of Lee's endless raving over the delicious meal, she made an appearance carrying her famous chocolate mousse on a silver tray, complete with powdered roses.

"Who're you?" Lee asked, looking first at Marie and then to me.

Before I could answer, Marie said, "Your wife's secret." Over our delectable dessert, I explained about Marie.

"You certainly know the way to a man's heart," Lee ribbed her as I took the dishes in.

"After-dinner drink?" I heard Lee ask Marie.

"Sounds good."

"Brandy?"

"Perfect."

When I heard Marie's throaty laugh, I knew they were becoming fast friends.

9

And Baby Makes Three: Big Career Change

When I was seven months pregnant, Lee went on a three-week location in Lone Pine to shoot a Western, *The Duel at Silver Creek*. This was our first real separation since our wedding. I was in nesting mode and spent my time shopping for a bassinet and buying baby clothes.

And then, out of the blue, I received a letter from Lee. He wrote that our marriage had been a mistake and he couldn't go through with it. I had to read the letter over and over again to take it all in. How could he have fallen out of love with me just like that? Maybe he never loved me to begin with, but whether he loved me or not, he didn't want to be saddled with a wife and child. After crying endlessly for a day or two while the news sank in, I wrote back, asking that he stay in the marriage until after the baby was born. There was no reply to that letter. I spent the next couple of weeks in despair, dreading his return.

He called when he got into Los Angeles and asked me to pick him up outside the Hollywood Roosevelt Hotel. His voice displayed no real emotion, and I had no idea what to expect as I drove there. I tried to stay calm as I pulled up to the curb. There was Lee, standing with his arms full of flowers. He jumped into the car and held me close, crushing the bouquet as he covered me with kisses. "What was I thinking?" he said. "I love you. I guess I just get scared sometimes. I'm sorry."

By the last month of my pregnancy I had gained more than fifty pounds. I could barely breathe, let alone sing, so I told Erv and Roger my career was going on hold indefinitely. Roger tried to convince me I could be a mom and still become a performer at MGM. Erv didn't try to convince me at all. He just cried. I cried too. But between becoming a mother and being married to an ambitious actor, I knew what I had to do. Besides, I had been raised to believe marriage and motherhood was the only important career for a woman.

As the due date drew near, I grew more anxious while Lee remained oblivious. My nose was buried in Dr. Spock half the time. I thought the first step to being a perfect mother was choosing the perfect name. I knew that if it were a boy, I would call him Christopher. My giving him the name of Joan Crawford's son, whom I had grown to love, was completely subconscious.

The last three weeks of my pregnancy Lee and I left halfway through a number of movies and raced to Queen Anne Hospital on false alarms. Finally it was the real thing. After a seventeen-hour ordeal trying to give birth with no success, I was wheeled into the delivery room and given an anesthetic.

I awoke very groggy, felt a sharp pain in my belly, reached down, and ran my hand over bandages wrapped tight around my swollen abdomen. I had never been in a hospital before and had been hoping for natural childbirth, not a long, painful labor ending with a cesarean.

A nurse came in to take my temperature and check my pulse. "Congratulations..You gave birth to a ten-pound baby boy."

"I can't believe it. No wonder I'm sore," I groaned. "My belly is so swollen I feel as if I'm still pregnant. When can I see him?"

"Now just relax. You need your rest."

"What's wrong? There's something you're not telling me. Where's my husband?"

"He called. Sends his love."

She disappeared and I drifted off. When I awakened again, Lee was scattering pink roses over my hospital bed. This was the first time I'd seen him since the morning before. I could see by his eyes and stubble of beard he had been out celebrating. Cigars fell from yesterday's shirt as he gently leaned over and gave me a kiss. "Wake up, sweetheart. We have a beautiful son." He handed me a rose. "Wrong color, but they don't come in blue."

"You can tell me, Lee. Please, I want the truth. What's wrong with the baby?"

"What? Sweetheart, listen to me. You had a big, healthy baby boy."

"So where is this baby? Why can't I see him?"

"You had a rough time and you have a slight fever. They don't want to take a chance of infection. Be patient, little mother. Move over. I'm exhausted." Before long he was snoring next to me on my narrow bed.

The night nurse came in, interrupted his nap, and sent him on his way. I fell back asleep.

I waited three days, full of doubts, but the appearance of Christopher Lamont Marvin, with a perfect head and no birthmarks, restored my confidence. Considering my own mother had been afraid to hold me, I was amazingly comfortable in this new mother role and couldn't stop kissing and marveling at my beautiful baby. When Lee and I brought him home from the hospital, it was one of the most exciting days of our lives.

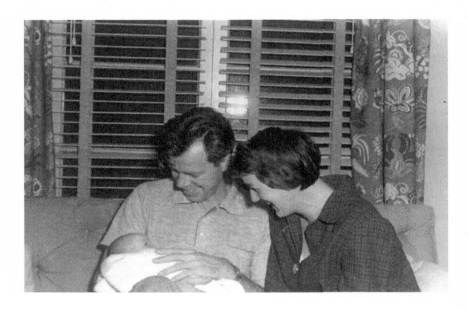

Marveling at baby Christopher, 1952

A week later Lee came into the bedroom, where I was taking a rest while Christopher napped. He had a martini in one hand and a cigarette in the other. "Hey, lazy. What are you doing in bed? It's the cocktail hour." He checked out the flowers that filled the room. There was a bouquet of white carnations from my mother and a pink azalea plant from Lee's family. The next card he read was attached to a bunch of white daisies in a blue china rabbit. It said, "Congratulations, Kiddo. I can't believe I'm a grandpa. Love, Daddy".

Lee put down his drink, went to the bassinet, and picked up little Christopher, enveloping him in smoke. "Come to Daddy, you little peanut."

When the baby started to cry, he quickly handed him to me. The crying stopped. Lee looked at the two of us. "Mother's magic touch . . . What about dinner? Want to go out?"

I couldn't believe my ears. "What about Christopher?"

"Throw him in a basket. We'll take him along."

I was speechless.

"I thought you'd like a change."

"That's all I do," I said. "This kid never stops peeing." I burst into tears and Lee looked at me helplessly. I was fighting to gain control. "Sorry. I can't seem to bounce back. I'm exhausted. Just when I get to sleep, he cries and I have to get up again."

"Funny, I never hear you."

"I try not to wake you. No point in both of us being up all night."

"Good thinking, sweetheart," he said. "Well, I'm gonna' run down to Ted's for a martini and a steak. I'll bring you back something." He gave me a kiss and was out the door.

10

Doris: The Woman Who Came to Dinner and Stayed

Children were not allowed in the Beverly Hills apartment, so a couple of weeks after our baby was born, Lee and I moved into a modest cottage in Beverly Glen and filled it with cheap contemporary furniture, including a new crib.

Shortly after moving, we were broke and had to borrow money against our one possession, the 1948 black Ford convertible. That car had saved us from bankruptcy before. It seemed every time we had to float a loan with the car as collateral Lee got a job. We decided it was our good luck charm and called it our "Black Ace in the Hole." Lo and behold, a week after we got the loan Lee got a tremendous break. He was cast as Chino, the heavy, opposite Marlon Brando in *The Wild One*.

As it happened, Brando lived close by. Once Lee became comfortable riding a motorcycle, Marlon, known as "Bud" to his family and friends, and Lee went to and from the studio on their bikes together.

"That guy tries to pick up every dame he sees at the stoplight," Lee said after their first outing together.

"Why?" I asked.

"He thinks it's fun. A game.

"And do you play?" I asked.

"Why should I?" said Lee, cuddling up to me. "I've got what I want right here."

Though Lee and Brando rode their bikes together and saw each other daily on the set, Brando was very introverted. It took a little while before he overcame his shyness and began spending time at our house. He loved playing the bongos and made a set of drums for me by punching holes in mason jars, then proceeded to teach me the finer points of drumming.

Soon he became part of our family and was Christopher's only babysitter. At first I was concerned about leaving the baby with Bud while Lee and I raced out to a movie, but they were both delighted with each other's company.

In fact, Marlon seemed happier playing with Christopher than spending time with adults. He started him drumming on anything and everything. When Christopher began crawling, Marlon would get down and crawl alongside him, imitating his sounds, repeating his words. When the baby saw Bud moving beside him and heard his own words coming back at him, he would fall over and giggle in delight. Marlon would do the same. What a pair.

I was hurriedly putting a fresh bunch of daisies into a glass pitcher one day when there was a knock at the door.

"Hey, kiddo!" Daddy embraced me. "Let's get a look at you."

Five-month-old Christopher had had his dinner, was in his sleepers, and fussing to get out of his playpen.

"Sorry, Daddy. Hi, Faye, just a minute—"

I picked up Christopher as he started to cry. Faye paid no notice. "Hi, honey," she said, smiling sweetly.

Daddy looked over at us. "I can't believe you're already a mother. You didn't waste any time, did you? Well, kiddo, at least you got married first. Where's the lucky guy? I can't wait to meet this movie star of yours."

"He's shooting. He'll be home soon." Juggling the baby on my hip, I went to make Daddy a martini the way Lee taught me and brought Faye a Coke. Christopher had stopped crying and, being a friendly child, was smiling and cooing. I was ready to pass him around, but neither his grandfather nor Faye seemed interested.

"I'm afraid I'd drop him," Daddy said, backing away.

"He's a fat little thing, isn't he?" Faye said, keeping her distance.

Neither of them had the slightest idea what to do with an infant, nor were they interested, so I excused myself and put him down for the night. When I returned Daddy nodded approvingly. "Looks like you're in your element. It's none of my business, but . . . can your husband support you and a baby? He doesn't even have a regular job."

"We get by. Right now he's playing a character in *The Wild One* with Marlon Brando. It's six weeks' work."

"What about the other forty-six?"

"His agent says he's got a great future. In this business you've got to have faith."

"Faith doesn't put food on the table, kiddo."

He should know, I thought. "Excuse me. I have to check the oven," I said, heading for the kitchen.

I was bringing in a plate of cheese and crackers when I heard Lee's motorcycle blasting up the hill.

Lee at home playing Chino from *The Wild One*, 1953

He charged through the front door, still in his leather biker costume from the movie, unshaven, chomping on a cigar butt. Behind him came a buxom brunette. *What on earth*! I bit my lip. A moment later I recognized her. She was yet another out-of-work actress we had met at a party a few weeks before. I had no idea what she was doing in our house.

Lee immediately went over to Daddy. "So, I finally get to meet the chief." Daddy, speechless, stood and they shook hands. Lee turned to Faye.

"Hello, lovely lady." He kissed her hand and she came undone. He waltzed over to me. "Hi, sweetheart." He gave me a long, passionate kiss, then, as an afterthought, acknowledged his companion. "Oh, you remember Doris, friend of Doug and Jane?"

I greeted her as pleasantly as possible. "Oh, hello. Nice to see you again."

"She needs a place to stay for the night," Lee said. "I told her she could crash on the sofa." Doris smiled at me while helping herself to the appetizers, and I halfheartedly smiled back. On his way to the makeshift bar, Lee checked Daddy's empty glass. "Hey, a martini man. Good. Let me fix you another . . . What about you, Doris?"

"I thought you'd never ask," Doris said coyly. She squeezed between Daddy and Faye while Lee made a pitcher of martinis for the three of them. I made my exit, going into the kitchen to finish preparing the meal. Lee came in to give me a hand.

"Where did Doris come from?" I asked immediately.

Lee put his arms around me. "Just a kid on the set with nowhere to stay. She'll be out of here tomorrow, I promise." He gave me a peck and went back into the living room.

We'd had a steady stream of overnight guests since our marriage. I told myself that one more was no big deal.

"Dinner!" I called, a little too shrilly. I brought a large, steaming platter of beef stroganoff on a bed of rice to the table.

Daddy looked like he'd hit the jackpot, with Faye seated on one side and Doris on the other. He took a bite and broke into a smile. "Delicious. Well, kiddo, you finally found your calling."

Doris laughed. "It's certainly not mine."

Daddy looked at her appreciatively. "No, you don't look like the domestic type." He looked at me and then at Lee, smiling. "It's great to see my little girl so happy. Can you afford her?"

Lee laughed. "Today I can."

Daddy nodded. "It's all in the luck of the draw. I've never had a nine-to-five job in my life. Couldn't take it. Nothing like a good roll of the dice to get the heart pumping. Course, the closest I've been to the Hollywood scene was once when I sat in on a weekly poker party at Louis B. Mayer's. Late in the game he was in the chips and one of the regulars accused him of cheating. 'How dare you insult me!' he yelled. 'I'm leaving here and never coming back.' He slammed the door behind him. Soon as he got outside, he realized he'd stormed out of his own house!" We all laughed.

Lee egged Daddy on. "Sounds like you've had some wild times."

"Oh, boy, have I," Daddy said. "I lost so much at the races one year I decided to join the winners and bought a track in Canada. Was the only year Canada got rained out the first season." Doris hung on my father's every word, but Daddy kept his eyes on Lee. "Tell me how you got the job with Brando," Daddy said.

"My agent got it. I had to lie and pretend I knew how to ride a motorcycle. First day I rode the damn thing through the women's john on the back lot. Now I love riding. Can't wait to get Betty her own bike so we can ride together."

That'll be the day! I thought.

At the end of the evening, we all walked outside together to say our good-byes. Doris whistled when she saw my father's sports car. Daddy gave her a wink, then turned to Lee. "Listen, son, you wanna make some real money, you talk to me. I just bought into a radium mine that's gonna be worth a fortune." He and Faye crawled into his pride and joy.

"When you're ready for one of these, you call the chief. You kids have gotta come over and check out my new digs in Beverly Hills. Real class. Bring some cash, Lee, and we'll shoot some pool." He fired up the engine and they sped off into the night.

Lee and I sat on the edge of our bed for twenty minutes waiting to brush our teeth while listening to Doris's version of "Why Don't You Do Right?" coming from our tiny bathroom. "Get out of here, and get me some money toooooo . . ." She sang loudly and off-key.

"One night, right?" I said, shaking my head.

The next morning Lee and I were up at dawn, he off to the studio, and I with our baby. Doris was sound asleep on the sofa, and her clothes were draped all over the living room. She slept through the morning as I fed Christopher and gave him his bath, washed his diapers and clothes in our old, used washing machine, hung them out to dry, put him down for his nap, then went out to work in the garden. After an early lunch I cleaned the house, purposely vacuuming the rug next to Doris. She never stirred, except to put a pillow over her head. Several hours later she got up, put on a Chinese silk robe, flipped on the radio, and made a pitcher of martinis, which accompanied her and the telephone into the bathroom. An hour later, she finally appeared in heavy makeup and a revealing cocktail dress, reeking of Joy perfume. "Well, I'm off to work," she said.

"Work?" I asked.

"Right now I'm making the rounds. Paramount tested me after I was crowned 'Miss Canada Dry.' Can you believe it? Me, 'Miss Canada Dry'?" A horn honked. "Gotta go, sweetie. There's my ride."

She passed Lee coming in. He went to the cupboard and picked up the empty gin bottle. "Goddamn it," he grumbled.

I went over, grabbed the car keys, and gave him a quick kiss. "I need money for the market."

"Don't talk to me about food," he joked. "There's not a drop to drink in the house."

"Doris's one night is over, as I see it," I said, going out the door. "Keep an eye on Christopher." The baby was in his playpen having a happy imaginary conversation on his toy telephone.

"Hurry back." Lee never wanted to be left alone with the baby.

Five days passed and Doris was still living at our house. She was like a fixture, part of the couch, until late afternoon, when men began calling her for last-minute dates. By that time we were both looking forward to bed, but for different reasons. Lee promised to tell her to leave, but she'd be gone when he came home, and we were always asleep when she came in at night.

I walked into the living room one morning and found her cheap, lacy under things strewn about the floor. I'd had it. "Rise and shine, Doris!" I shouted into her ear. In a fog she took off her sleep mask and fumbled for a cigarette.

"What time is it?" she groaned.

"Time to pack," I said. I had her up and out of the house before Lee got home from the studio. We celebrated by popping our one bottle of champagne and making love on our reclaimed sofa.

*   *   *

As attractive and charismatic as he was, there was a side to my new husband that surfaced night after night in his sleep. He was plagued with terrible nightmares about his time in the Marines during World War Two. Many nights I was up changing the sheets wet with sweat, which poured from memories he forced himself to turn off while awake. Like many damaged war heroes—Lee had received the Purple Heart—he clung to the pride of having been a Marine. Then he drank to forget what the war had done to him.

*　　*　　*

11

Movies, Baby, Movies, Baby, and So On

After *The Wild One* wrapped, Brando returned to New York. When he was leaving Beverly Glen, we promised to stay in touch and get together. But, as often happens when filming ends, we drifted apart. I missed not having him around, particularly for our drumming sessions. Christopher kept looking for him whenever he went crawling.

When we got to the theater for the opening of *The Wild One*, we were thrown into total chaos. It was almost New Year's Eve—December 30, 1953—and word of the film (then called *Hot Blood*) had gotten out to the Hells Angels. They'd seen previews and had already crowned Lee their new hero, and they were there to party. The front of the theater was jammed with bikers in full regalia on their motorcycles, their tough-looking girlfriends behind them. When they saw Lee they went crazy.

"Chino! Chino!" they chanted, calling out his character's name over and over again. Lee waved, put his arm around me, and guided me past the mob.

"Don't look at them," he whispered.

But following the evening of the screening, it was impossible to avoid them. They began to follow us, and it was frightening when they would appear unexpectedly. Lee mentioned a few had even shown up when he was riding his dirt bike on some back trails.

One weekend we left Christopher with a baby sitter and hauled the motorcycle out to the desert so Lee could participate in an all-day "hair and hound." We had rented a cabin nearby at Big Bear. After driving Lee and his bike out to the starting lineup of the race, I went back to the cabin and found it full of Hells Angels. They must have followed us and taken over our small getaway while I was gone. They were hanging out with their "douche bags," as they called their female counterparts. Nobody budged when I came through the door. They were too busy guzzling beer and laughing raucously at their own crude jokes. They clearly had no intention of leaving. I was terrified.

Without making eye contact, I managed a nervous "Hi", and raced into the makeshift kitchen. *When in doubt, cook*, I told myself. I grabbed everything I'd brought for our weekend away and got busy heating chili, hot dogs, and anything else I could quickly get my hands on. From the kitchen, over the radio blaring rock and roll, I could hear a lot of "Fuck", "Shit, man," and "Oh, baby." When I came in with refreshments, I saw a lot of dirty dancing going on. I kept reassuring the guys—and myself—that Lee would back any minute.

In the late afternoon he finally walked in the door. Hells Angels froze. Lee sized up the situation, walked over and turned down the radio, then got himself a beer and raised it high. The guests let out a cheer. They crowded around him, but Lee gently pushed them aside, taking me by the hand into the bedroom and closing the door.

"Did any of these guys touch you?"

"Nobody touched me. They forgot I was here." Lee, always the actor, managed to have a quick beer with his "fans" and sent them on their way.

Lee came into the kitchen one morning when I was feeding Christopher. He poured himself a cup of coffee, made a face at the baby, and joined us.

"Sweetheart, what about this? We'll pack up the car and take a trip up the coast. I've never been to Oregon, and it's about time I meet your mother."

I was reluctant. "Can you take the time?"

"I need a break. We'll take a family tour. It'll be fun."

Not for me, I thought. A family tour indeed. I imagined my mother with Lee—let alone my stepfather and Lee—and cringed. I hadn't told Lee much about my unhappy childhood, being abandoned by both parents. I was ashamed of my early life.

"Are you sure you want to drive that distance with a baby in the car?"

"Come on, sweetheart. Call your mom and tell her we're coming. I've met your crazy daddy. Now it's time to meet the other half."

"Can we go on to Washington and see my grandparents?"

"Sure, I've been dying to meet your aunt Rella."

Even though I hated the idea of spending time with my mother and Elburn, I wanted to show off my devoted husband and beautiful baby. I wanted my mother to see Lee loving me and my giving Christopher the kind of care she had been incapable of giving me. I told myself if I could get through that visit I would have the payoff of spending time with Grandma and Grandpa Rundquist, the family who had raised me. So I gave in and called my mother.

"I told my mother we could only stay three days, okay?"

Lee put his arms around me. "We'll only stay three hours if you like. Whatever you want. Don't worry, sweetheart. You have me, remember? We're a team."

At that moment I loved my husband more than ever.

My mother was watching and waiting for us at the front door. She was still pretty, though much heavier than when I'd last seen her six years before. Even though she was wearing a matronly cotton housedress with an apron, she had kept her hair dyed the original auburn. After greeting me warmly, she became as shy as a schoolgirl when meeting Lee. She blushed when he kissed her cheek and called her "Mother," still a moth to the flame when it came to any male attention.

Mother in 1953

Just as I had guessed, she seemed to be in awe of Christopher the whole visit. Like a child, she watched my every move as I bathed him, fed him, changed him, and played with him. She even got up her nerve to hold him briefly.

The three days passed slowly, and I was relieved when our time there was over.

"See you soon," my mother and I said to each other as Lee and I went to the car. It wouldn't be soon. She and Fat were back inside the house before we'd even left the driveway.

After the three of us were safely back in the security of our car heading to my childhood home, I burst into tears. Lee pulled to the side of the road, turned off the engine, and held me.

"I know that was hard, honey, but we did the right thing. You were wonderful. And your mother loves you. She just can't show it. She's like a little girl."

"Swell," I sniffled. "Little girls should play with dolls and not have babies."

By contrast, our visit with Grandma and Grandpa Rundquist was a pleasure. My seventy-seven-year-old grandfather and Lee were kindred spirits. They both loved fishing and were on the lake or river every morning at daybreak. Lee was amazed at my grandfather's energy. "He's the youngest man I've ever met," Lee observed.

My father's family was duly impressed with my husband's acting career and put on a formal feast to welcome their new family member. For the first time in my life I did not feel like the poor relative. Aunt Rella was in rare form and played the piano nonstop.

On our drive back to California, I realized it had been good to go home again. I had left eight years before with nothing but hope and determination for a better life. So far my good fortune was beyond my wildest dreams, and the future held great promise.

When Lee was sent the script for *The Big Heat*, we sat up in bed reading it together. Fritz Lang was set to direct, and the screenplay was raw and powerful. It was also funny—Lee and I laughed out loud at Gloria Grahame's line when she walks into a dismal hotel room, looks around, and says, "Oh. This is great; early nothing." Lee's role, Vince Stone, called on him to play a sadistic gangster who turns on her. When we got to the scene where Lee was to throw boiling coffee in her face, disfiguring her, I shuddered.

"Bit over the top, isn't it?" Lee asked, an eyebrow raised at me.

"Everyone will remember that scene, I promise you."

"Script's good, though."

"Meyer's right, Lee. This will be good for your career."

Meyer Mishkin had been Lee's agent for almost five years, taking him on when Lee was twenty-five, and we trusted him for good reason. He worked hard for Lee; moreover, instead of the usual Hollywood smugness, he had New York City smarts, which Lee counted as gold.

Almost immediately after Lee left to start work on *The Big Heat*, I learned I was expecting again. Jerry was over a few hours after I'd gotten the news, and Christopher was toddling back and forth between us, pulling at Jerry's shoelaces.

"Cute," said Jerry wryly.

"Good thing you think so. He's going to have a little brother or sister in a few months."

"God, Betty, that's just obscene!" Jerry shook his head, laughing. "When are you not pregnant?"

It was true. When Christopher was just a couple of months old, I lost a baby to an early miscarriage. Now he was a year old, and I was with child once again. I was happy but nervous, especially after the miscarriage. Lee, on the other hand, was thrilled.

"The more the merrier," he sang when I told him.

After *The Big Heat*, Lee was scheduled to go to Mexico to shoot *Gorilla at Large*, which seemed like a silly project to me, a thriller being filmed in 3-D. At least he had only one line. It was a short location, and he'd get to work with Lee J. Cobb and Raymond Burr. A beautiful young actress, Anne Bancroft, was the female lead. That didn't hurt either.

Lee left for Mexico, promising to be back quickly, as our second child was due in just weeks. Two days before I expected him home, the phone rang in the middle of the night.

"Hi, baby. Did I wake you?"

It was 2 AM, and he sounded like he'd had a couple. But it was still good to hear his voice.

"Hi, darling. It's okay. I miss you."

"I miss you, too, but I'm afraid I'm gonna be later getting home than I thought."

"Why?"

"Shoot's delayed. You won't believe it, sweetheart. We've run out of film! Shooting in Mexico is a joke!"

Lee was home when, right on schedule, in the spring of 1954, another cesarean brought Courtenay Lee Marvin, a beautiful daughter with a perfect head and no birthmarks.

With this new addition to the family, we'd run out of space in our rented cottage. "We'll have to move," I told Lee.

"Start looking for a house to buy," he said. "I've got two more films lined up after this one."

Lee's steady work gave us enough money for a down payment on our first home, a new, three-bedroom California ranch house in the Hollywood

Knolls. There was even enough left over for me to furnish our new home with reproductions of French country furniture.

I wanted to have a housewarming. Lee was amenable, but I sensed he was doing it for me. "Doing the 'Keeping up with the Joneses' thing," he teased, circling his arms around me. "Sure, let's warm up the place."

I sent out invitations for our first cocktail party. Roger and Jerry were there as well as my friend Robert, who had been named Christopher's godfather. It was fun to look around and see the mix of people, from old friends to new acquaintances, mostly Hollywood hopefuls. Knowing we had a toddler, a couple of people had brought their own kids, and there were babies crawling around in the mix of things. I kept the buffet table filled while Lee made drinks and held court.

At their bedtime, I brought Christopher and Courtenay over to Daddy for a goodnight kiss. Daddy was definitely drunk. Later in the evening the party was winding down, but the remaining guests showed no signs of leaving. On my way to the kitchen to refill an empty platter, I spied Lee off by himself in a corner. He was barely holding onto a full drink, eyes half-closed. When I came back from the kitchen he was gone.

I declared the party over. By the time I crawled into bed, Lee was still nowhere to be found. A couple of hours later, I was awakened by a popping noise, like the sound of a firecracker. Still no Lee. I lay there for a while, then went out in my bathrobe and found him asleep at the wheel of his MG, parked in our driveway. He was cradling a Colt .45, one of the precious guns from his collection. I climbed in next to him, and he opened his eyes. "Oh, Mommy," he murmured, "I shot the house." The next day he was out patching two bullet holes in the side of our new home

We were in the midst of an eight-year stretch that, unbeknown to us at the time, would feature baby, movies, baby, movies, again and again. In fact, Meyer kept Lee so busy my husband was often shooting two or three pictures a year.

The Big Heat opened to much acclaim, and, just as we expected, Lee's coffee pot scene with Gloria Grahame was the talk of every tabloid and industry paper. The intensity of Lee's performance was gaining him a reputation as someone fearsome and formidable. When an interviewer asked me, "How do you live with a man like that?" I had to laugh.

"It's easy," I said. "Inside that tough exterior, Lee Marvin's just a big bowl of mashed potatoes."

Behind the scenes that was true. Most of the time he was loving, attentive, and surprisingly gentle. We grabbed any time we could get to be alone together, but my days were filled with the demands of two babies.

Mouseketeers Christopher and Courtenay, 1956

Lee adored our children, but he couldn't figure out what to do with them. He knew what to do with any character handed to him in a film script—he became that character effortlessly—but in between films he could play the role of father for only brief bits of time. Then he needed to get out of the house, go drinking with his buddies, or take off on his motorcycle. I tried to let this go, too busy and tired from young motherhood to think about what was beginning to surface in my husband.

I figured he would become more comfortable with the children as they got older. But he was jealous of them. He wanted me for himself. When he was shooting *Pete Kelly's Blues* at the Warner Brothers Studio, just a few months after I'd given birth to Courtenay, he started asking me to come to the set. "Can't you just be there for me, honey?" he'd ask late at night, when we finally had some time to ourselves. "Gives me a good feeling to know you're around." That was fine, but we had a four-month-old daughter and a little boy not yet two.

I found a sitter, and finally made it to the studio where Lee was shooting "Pete Kelly's Blues". In the film Lee was playing the best friend of Jack Webb, fresh off "*Dragnet*". Webb was directing as well as starring, and it wasn't easy for Lee to take direction from his co-star. That afternoon, when I was on the set, I kept a sharp eye on my watch even though the studio was less than a mile from our house. I had promised the baby sitter I'dto be gone no longer than two hours. I didn't realize that once the light outside the set door went red, absolutely nobody could enter or leave and I was trapped until we heard "Cut" and "Print.". The scene was short, but they just couldn't get it. "Again," I'd hear Webb say, after each take., "Again."

After three hours I was in a panic. I had to get home. I signaled frantically to Lee, but to no avail. He was having problems of his own. Finally I had a production assistant go up between takes and whisper in his ear. Lee took a break and I bolted out of there. Our lives were definitely in two different places.

Taking a much-needed break in Hawaii, 1956

Lee's star was rising, and he was going after success with a passion. He loved acting and cared deeply about the quality of his work, but he didn't like the notoriety. He'd get edgy when life got "too Hollywood." He'd rather be out drinking late with the crew than seeking the limelight at celebrity spots. Many nights I was asleep by the time he got home. I didn't like going to bed alone, but it was part of our lifestyle, and I supported his career 100 percent.

When director John Sturges cast him as Hector David in *Bad Day at Black Rock*, Lee was over the moon. He'd be working with one of his idols, Spencer Tracy. In fact, the project had a dream cast, including Ernest Borgnine, Anne Francis, Walter Brennan, and Robert Ryan.

Lee once again asked me to join him on location. By this time I had a regular sitter, lovely Nanny Lilly. I left Christopher and Courtenay in her care and drove 175 miles to Lone Pine, a small, one-street town located between the High Sierras and Death Valley—one of the most picturesque and popular locations for Westerns. It was a hot night when I arrived, and I heard the beetles crunching under my tires as I searched for the modest motel where the cast was staying. Lee was happy to see me and couldn't wait to tell me about working with Spencer Tracy.

"He's amazing, sweetheart. When I watch him work I realize I have so much to learn. Yesterday Ernie Borgnine got a real lesson. He'd been telling me how he was going to take a scene away from Tracy—Spencer Tracy—can you believe it? There's a scene where Spence comes up to Borgnine in front of the hotel and starts to ask directions. Ernie gets this bright idea to take out a toothpick and start picking his teeth. Well, when Tracy sees that, he takes a handkerchief out of his pocket and keeps mopping his forehead. Steals the scene. I'm telling you, honey, in my scene with Tracy, I'm doing nothing. Not one bit of business. Nada."

The next day I watched Lee shoot his big scene. Propped up on a bed in a sleazy motel room, he greeted Spencer Tracy with great hostility, delivering his lines without moving a muscle. He was ice. Mr. Tracy was impressed. He came over to Lee after the first take and said, "This is your scene, kid. Take it."

It was a great day for Lee.

Everything seemed to be getting better and better. And soon thereafter I was pregnant once again.

"What's this?" Lee asked as I handed him a big box tied with a red ribbon on Valentine's Day.

"Open it."

"Okay, okay!"

At first he looked stunned, then he broke into a big smile. "Is it too silly? Will you wear it?" I asked.

"Are you kidding? This is great. I'm never taking it off. I'm wearing it to bed."

Lee put on the white motorcycle crash helmet sporting two cherry red, interlocked hearts with our initials.

He pulled me to him. I could tell he had only one thing on his mind, but I had to ask him, "Are you sure you're okay with another baby?"

"Better than okay. I love you pregnant." He was kissing me harder, the helmet pushing into my forehead.

"Lee . . ."

He danced me out of the living room and toward our bedroom.

"I told you, I'm wearing it to bed. Come here, you."

"Close the door! The kids!"

He kicked the door shut and grabbed me. "Happy Valentine's Day, sweetheart." He frantically tore off all our clothes but kept the helmet on the whole time we made love.

Keenan Wynn came over the next day to go riding, despite the unusually cold weather. Lee and Keenan had met when shooting *Shack Out on 101* and hit it off easily. They were both fixated on their motorcycles and went out riding every chance they got. I came in from driving the children to nursery school and found him waiting for Lee, double vodka in hand. It was about ten AM.

"Little early, isn't it?"

"Not by my time." He extended his arm and I looked at his watch. Each number was a five.

"Cocktail hour!" He downed his drink and poured a second, lighter one.

Lee came in, joined Keenan in a quick eye-opener, then kissed me good morning and good-bye.

"Somebody loooves you," I heard Keenan ribbing him, following behind as Lee put on his crash helmet, the two painted hearts gleaming in the sun.

12

Meet the In-Laws: One Crazy Family

I felt queasy during our three-hour drive from LaGuardia Airport through the Catskills, not knowing if it was my pregnancy or the anticipation of visiting Lee's family on their terrain. Our daughter Courtenay, her grandmother's namesake, was asleep on my lap. Christopher, now four, was getting restless. "Mommy, Mommy," he whined, trying to crawl into the front seat. "Hold me, hold me."

"I can't hold you, honey. I'm holding Courtenay." I was seven months pregnant, so holding her was a challenge.

His fussing woke Courtenay and she began to cry. I had run out of treats and stories and was almost out of patience.

"No. No . . . Mommy, you hold me!" He had his arms around my neck. "No more ride. I want out."

Lee slammed on the breaks, jumped out of the car, and opened the back door. "You want out? Then get out!"

Christopher began to cry as Lee slammed the back door and walked away. I put Courtenay in the back and followed him. "I can't take it anymore! I'm not cut out for this!" he yelled. "Can't you shut them up?"

"Lee, calm down," I pleaded. "We only have another thirty minutes to go. You're acting like the child!"

I went back to the car to console my other, younger babies and let them share what was left of my lap. Lee joined us shortly, apologized, and we completed our journey without further incident.

We arrived in Woodstock and drove up the long driveway to the back of a formal, white Colonial house set on a beautiful knoll surrounded by neighboring farms. Lee's father and brother were waiting by the back door to greet us. Lamont Marvin came to the car. "Welcome," he said warmly.

He lifted Christopher and Courtenay out of the back. "Well, look at you two. I've waited a long time for this. I'm your grandfather Monty." Lee and his father shook hands.

I struggled to get out of the car. Lee hoisted me up and led me over to his brother, Robert, fair and thin with red hair and glasses. Lee overpowered him with a big hug. "I want you to meet my best friend and most severe critic, my wife."

"Hello, Betty," Robert stammered.

The children and I held hands as we passed through the formal dining room into the parlor, furnished with velvet settees and small marble tables covered with lace doilies and delicate china. On seeing this, I held their little hands more tightly. Mother Courtenay, in a petite, black silk dress, was seated in a gold silk brocade Queen Anne chair by the fireplace, near an antique harp. She held her head high, eyes hidden behind thick glasses, not a silver-blond hair out of place. She lifted a long, ivory cigarette holder to her lips and took a puff, showing off her Chinese red nails and matching lipstick. She turned her head in my direction and spoke with a deep, thick, Southern accent. "You look like you've had a rough journey."

"Hello, Mother Courtenay," I said and reached down to give her a kiss. She turned her cheek. The children began to explore. "May I put this out of reach?" I asked, picking up a figurine from a nearby table.

"Please don't touch my things," she said.

"Sorry!" I put it down, grabbed the babies, and stood frozen to the spot. After what seemed like an eternity, Lee came into the room.

"Hello, darling!" Mother Courtenay exclaimed as she opened her arms to receive his embrace.

"What do you think of my family?" Lee asked.

"I'd think you were Catholic. How many of these do you plan on having?" she said, eyeing the children and my burgeoning belly. I excused myself and went upstairs with my brood to unpack, wondering how we would make it through the week.

The next day was Easter Sunday. After church, many of the congregation lined up for Lee to autograph their programs. Robert stood off to the side, glaring at his brother. Lee was congenial to his fans, but I could tell he wanted out. I gently touched his elbow, smiled to the crowd, and steered him toward the car.

"Bless you, my child," he intoned, kissing me on the lips as we walked away. Robert was behind us, sullen and silent.

The moment we returned home, Lamont wheeled the liquor cart into the living room. Mother Courtenay took her place in her chair while he fixed her a double Jack Daniel's, neat, in a crystal goblet. Next came a pitcher of dry Beefeaters martinis for the men. Because of my condition I abstained, which I'm sure was another mark against me.

Lamont somehow managed to get a leg of lamb surrounded by potatoes, onions, and carrots into the oven while tending bar. I sat at one end of the room with the children, holding Courtenay and reading to Christopher. I could hear the men trading crude war stories, so I raised my voice to drown them out. After more martinis and a second double for Mother Courtenay, the group stumbled to the dinner table. "Monty" took Mother Courtenay's arm, as she was visibly weaving. I cautiously brought in the children and put them into borrowed high chairs next to me.

Lamont carved the lamb and passed the platter. He opened a bottle of wine and, in a sentimental moment, began a toast. "To our darling Betty, the daughter I always wanted. We are so happy—"

Mother Courtenay interrupted. "What are you talking about? You never mentioned any such thing to me, wanting a daughter. I guess now you love her more than me." She shed a tear and Monty ran over to comfort her.

"Robert's the daughter you always wanted," Lee joked. "He was always dressing up in Mother's clothes."

"At least I wasn't fucking every bimbo in town," Robert snapped.

"You son of a bitch!" Lee yelled, jumping up, grabbing the leg of lamb off the platter, and hurling it at his brother's head. Robert ducked.

"Yay, Daddy!" shouted Courtenay, clapping her hands and throwing her carrots at Christopher. Christopher laughed gleefully and tossed a handful of potatoes back at her.

Mother Courtenay attempted to assert herself. "Boys! Boys! Sit down and behave yourselves." Lee took his seat, grimacing, but Robert, ignoring his mother, stood and left the room.

"More!" my daughter was squealing, still flinging bits of food at her brother. Recovering from my shock at the outrageous scene that just took place, I was about to discipline my kids when Mother Courtenay turned and looked at me disapprovingly. "Can't you control your children?"

The table fell silent. She gazed at her plate and spoke quietly to her husband. "Monty, the meat is overcooked. You know I like it medium rare." The leg of lamb lay on the floor behind her, grease dripping onto the Persian rug.

"Sorry, dear," said Monty.

She held out her empty wine glass and he refilled it. "Thank you, dear," she said dismissively.

Lee turned on his mother. "You are a first-class bitch."

"Don't speak that way to your mother," Lamont said.

"Damn it, Chief, why do you let her get away with that crap?"

"Don't speak that way to your father," Mother Courtenay said.

"You know, you make me sick." Robert's voice came from behind us. He had returned, double martini in hand, and was standing in the doorway, glaring at Lee. "I don't care who you think you are. You have no business coming in here and upsetting my family!"

Lee stood up, suddenly sober. "Don't worry. It won't happen again." He took my hand. "Come on, honey, let's go."

"I really hate that woman," he said with constraint as we drove back to Manhattan. He gripped the wheel, and I could see he was doing everything in his power to keep from exploding. Thank God the kids had fallen asleep. I put my hand on his thigh and gave it a squeeze. He shook his head and sighed. "Do you know what she had the nerve to ask me while you were upstairs packing? She asked me what I really knew about you." He took my hand. "My darling mother thinks you married me because you knew I was going to be a star. Can you believe that bitch?"

I was too stunned to answer.

13

Homes, Sweet Homes: Moving On Up

In June 1956, when our daughter Cynthia came into the world, my college roommate Bev called from New York. She had married Joe, a dancer-choreographer on Broadway, and had given birth to her daughter, Tracy, the day after I delivered Cynthia. I was pleased our lives continued to parallel each other.

College roommate Beverly, 1956

That summer Lee was taking a brief break from making films to play File in *The Rainmaker* at the La Jolla Playhouse. I went to spend time with him and take a much-needed rest. Lee and I became friendly with the show's producers, the actress Dorothy McGuire and her husband, John Swope, and the cast, including James Whitmore and Theresa Wright. Jim's wife, Nancy, joined us, and she and I became friends for life. We all had great fun in that little town, hanging out at the Whale Room Bar, away from the tension of Hollywood life—just a bunch of stage actors drinking in the evening and swapping stories. Lee and I ended each night cuddling in bed, more like young lovers than the parents of three children.

After we returned to Los Angeles, Jim and Nancy invited us to dinner at their charming home at the end of Latimer Road in Uplifter's Ranch. We had trouble finding our way through that old state tree farm, and by midnight we were lost trying to find our way out. The eucalyptus and oak trees seemed to stretch out for miles. We were thrilled to discover this rural paradise. It was like being in New England—in the middle of Los Angeles, no less.

While Lee was away on location with *Raintree County* in Kentucky, Theresa Wright, one of the guests at dinner, invited me to lunch at her home, also in Uplifter's Ranch.

"I can't tell you how much I love this place," I said to her, looking around her charming cottage as we dined on the back patio. "It's not like anywhere else."

"Come on," Theresa said after lunch, "let's take a walk. I'm dying to look around Johnny Weismuller's house. It's up for sale."

We passed a row of eclectic houses, no two alike. When we walked by a log cabin next to an old California cottage, Theresa told me the story of Uplifter's Ranch. "In 1913 mostly artists and writers lived here. In 1921 it was taken over by the jolly band of the Uplifters, a group of wealthy L.A. business men, including Hollywood producers. They built a clubhouse, vacation cottages and a private polo field. But over ten years ago, the state turned it into a public park.

"Actually," she smiled, "that's a bit of a secret. We don't tell anyone it's a public park. We still own the roads and keep potholes in them so traffic has to slow down for the kids."

Theresa stopped in front of an old house overrun with weeds and vines crawling up the sides of the fenced property.

"This is it."

We peered through the back gate of the Weismuller home, at 2 Latimer Road.

"If Johnny Weissmuller lived here, wouldn't you think there'd be a pool?" I asked. Theresa laughed.

Beryl Ginter, the former Mrs. Weismuller, caught us peeking and invited us in. The interior of the spacious house, though in complete disrepair, was full of charm. I fell in love with the place.

I called Lee in Kentucky.

"I've found our perfect home, a big, old, two-story bastard Victorian. And guess where? In the old Uplifter's Ranch! We'll never have to move again, no matter how many more kids we have!" I was talking a mile a minute.

"Fine, honey, show it to Ed."

I asked Ed Silver, our conservative business manager, to take a look at my new love. He was not impressed. He called Lee and told him the house was a mess, definitely a bad investment.

"Does Betty want it?" Lee asked him.

"Yes."

"Then buy it."

We had found our fourth and final home.

The Latimer Road house needed a lot of work, but it had good bones. While Lee was still away on *Raintree County*, I took the children with me every day to work on the place, patching holes in the walls before they could be painted, scrubbing the filthy bathrooms, and hauling endless bags of trash off the premises. When Lee returned two weeks later, it was nowhere nearly finished, but I had made a lot of progress. He took one look around and called the place a dump, and I burst into tears.

But I persevered. With a limited budget and tremendous effort, I turned the house into an ideal home for our family. The kids had their own specially built and decorated bedrooms and baths, a huge playroom across our courtyard, and a large playhouse built in the garden. When it came to the master bedroom, Lee told me to be creative. I got carried away, and the room ended up with pink silk walls and a hand-carved *M* on the headboard. Some men might have found pink silk a little feminine, but Lee thought it sexy. "It's a boudoir, for Christ's sake. It should be feminine." I loved his sense of style.

We had a big housewarming and filled the house with new neighbors and friends, including Keenan's father, Ed Wynn. Ed was unique. He gave me a gift of a rug featuring the Texaco sign from his TV series. Like a fool I threw it out, not realizing that one day it would be a collector's item.

Not long after Lee came home, I became pregnant again. When Dr. Mishell gave me the news, I cried. I was already in way over my head, taking care of three children under the age of six and seeing to the needs of a demanding husband. But I knew how much Lee loved my being pregnant and our having children. I would have been happier about having another baby if only Lee had taken some responsibility for the kids. But that was a losing battle.

One Sunday afternoon he and Keenan were in the bar doing what they liked to do best. I had to run to the market.

"Darling, would you watch the babies? They're playing in the courtyard. I'll be back in twenty minutes.

"Absolutely."

When I returned, Courtenay and Christopher were nowhere in sight. Finding them wasn't hard. I just followed a trail of flour, chocolate syrup, and sugar into the kitchen.

"Mommy!" Courtenay called. "Don't come in! We're fixing you a surprise!" They were trying to make a cake. The floor was littered with eggshells and puddles of batter, and there were chocolate handprints all over the counter and the cabinets. Both Courtenay and Christopher were covered in goop. "Oh, no!" I yelled. Lee must have heard me, because he came ambling in. I blew up.

"The kids have made a terrible mess! I thought you were watching them!"

"I was."

"Look at the kitchen!"

"Well, I thought they were fine."

"You're impossible!" I yelled, rushing the kids into the bathroom to clean them off.

"What's the matter, sweetheart?" he called after me.

Lee just didn't get it. Or he didn't want to get it. Either way I figured I could manage without his support. But things were about to change more than either of us could imagine.

"So how did it go?" I asked Lee as he came into the playroom, tugging at his tie. He threw it over the armchair, unbuttoned his shirt at the neck, and sat down, running his hands through his salt-and-pepper hair.

"It's a lot of money."

"As in . . . ?" I tried to keep my voice casual. But his meeting with MCA, at the time the world's largest and most successful entertainment agency, was a big deal. The agency had a television series in mind for Lee, but we really didn't know much else about it. Lee had tried to play it cool when he left in the morning, but we both knew the stakes could turn out to be high.

"As in, well, a million dollars, sweetheart. They offered me a million dollars."

We stared at each other for a moment. Nobody had ever been offered a million-dollar television contract.

"Well, what did you say?"

"What do you think I said?" Suddenly both of us were laughing.

"Jesus, sweetheart, get me a drink!" Lee said. "Isn't this the craziest thing? It's a cop show. A million bucks for a friggin cop show—*M Squad*."

"What does the *M* stand for?"

"Murder. As in, 'The schedule for this series will be 'Murder.'"

I sat on the arm of Lee's chair, rubbing his neck. "What about Meyer?"

Lee's face turned somber. Meyer Mishkin had discovered him, backed him, and had been not only his agent but his staunch supporter from the beginning. "The guys at the meeting, Lew Wasserman, the head honcho, said something I've been thinking myself. Meyer's great. We've had a fast ride together, but he only sees me as playing the heavy. MCA sees me as a leading man."

Neither of us said anything for a moment.

"It's time for a change," Lee said finally. "I'll get Meyer to understand . . . Where's that drink?"

I knew Lee doing a series meant he would be gone long hours, but at least he would not be on location and we would have our weekends. We were looking for a way to spend more time together as a family and had learned that, except for running down the hill to our favorite neighborhood joint for a steak or hamburger, it was increasingly difficult to go out in public together. A few months before we had taken the children to Disneyland, which turned into a fiasco. Fans literally pulled Lee away from the kids, who ended up in tears. We were out of there in less than an hour. We needed a private place to play.

Keenan and his wife, Sharley, had bought a mountain cabin in Wrightwood, a three-hour drive from Los Angeles, and convinced us it was the perfect place to get away to on weekends and holidays. We were charmed by the community and ended up buying Turtle Lodge, a big, rustic log structure on an acre of land covered with giant pine trees. It had a beamed living room with stone fireplace, a country kitchen, and three bedrooms, two of which were loaded with bunk beds. This was a perfect family retreat with no telephone, TV, or radio. I was confident getting away as a family would help keep our marriage on track.

Turtle Lodge

On Fridays after school, in a station wagon loaded down with provisions, including our Hungarian Puli puppy, I picked up the children—and many times their friends—and drove to the lodge. Lee would drive directly from the studio and join us later in the evening. Except for the rare times he strayed to the bar, he would be with us for a late supper.

We loved being out of touch with the rest of the world, listening to records, reading and telling stories by the fire. We practiced a pioneer life: Lee cut firewood, and I baked bread and knitted sweaters. When the first snowfall covered the mountain, we all learned to ski, becoming friends with the local instructors. Turtle Lodge quickly turned into the favorite gathering spot for skiers, many of whom filled the bunk beds. There was plenty of food, wine, and song. The Twist was the rage, so we skied all day and twisted the night away.

The first season I found myself spending endless hours in the kitchen, cooking and cleaning up after the others had left for the slopes. I got smart and made a rule that no one skied before the hostess. Help was immediately available.

At the lodge the children, who adored their father, never felt neglected. When he was away from the pressures of the business, he could be fantastic fun. Some Sunday mornings he'd get up early, turn on the hi-fi full blast, and march through the lodge, waking us all to join his "Scottish Marching Band." Lee loved music, particularly early blues. When the mood struck, he would fill the place with Leadbelly, Bunk Johnson or Wee Bee Booze. Coming up behind me in the kitchen, he'd grab my butt while the children giggled, then he'd shuffle me from one end of the room to the other, whispering into my ear, "If you don't love this music, you're undersexed."

Our time at the lodge was paradise, and I tried to carry that spirit of fun off the mountain and transplant it into our Latimer Road home.

One Sunday afternoon in early December I sat on the stairs watching a bunch of Lee's biker buddies, dressed in black leathers, sprawled out on the white carpet in our formal living room, guzzling beer out of cans, trying to outmatch each other with stories.

"You know, you'll just be looking at smoke if you try to race me."

"My hog takes your old Harley any day."

This was a special clan, a closed club. They even exchanged photos of themselves in their gear with their bikes.

I decided they needed a new member. A big guy. By now I was six months into my fourth pregnancy and in perfect shape to disguise myself as one of them. Jerry helped me haul Lee's dirt bike across the road, where I posed for his camera, slouched on the bike in Lee's leathers and helmet, with a beer can in one hand, my head down to partially hide my face. On Christmas Day each of Lee's "gang got an unsigned, framed photograph.

Lee opened his anonymous gift and passed it to me.

"Who is this guy?"

I looked over. "Don't know him," I said, going back to the children and their presents.

"Well, he doesn't look like any of the guys I ride with."

That afternoon, Keenan came over, and Lee popped a bottle of Dom Perignon from the case he had bought to get him through the holidays. Keenan passed on the champagne and went behind the bar for a glass of his usual Stoli. He spotted the photo of me on the bike.

"Who in the hell is this character? I got one of these too," Keenan asked.

"Beats the hell out of me," Lee said.

As I passed through the room, picking up the Christmas wrappings from that morning, Lee looked up and suddenly grabbed me.

"Stay right there, Betty."

"Can't. I have to check on the turkey," I said, trying to get away and avoid his eyes so I wouldn't burst out laughing. Lee studied the picture and then looked intently at me. He turned to Keenan.

"See any similarity?" Keenan was still looking puzzled as Lee smiled, shook his head, put his arms around me, and gave me a big kiss. "You're too much, sweetheart."

14

There's No Such Thing as a Little Lie

We were being transported in a black stretch limousine up Hollywood Boulevard to Grauman's Chinese Theatre for the premiere of *Cat on a Hot Tin Roof*. I studied Lee's profile: the nearly silver hair, rather short and wide upturned nose, and strong jaw full of recently capped teeth. He was a handsome sight in a black tux—his monkey suit, as he called it. I was wearing a black Peau de Soie maternity gown, created for me by my then favorite designer, Jimmy Galanos. A white fox stole was draped over my bare shoulders.

Lee reached over to the bar to replenish his drink. This would make his third, since he'd already had a drink before we left the house. (When did I start counting?) I closed the partition between us and the driver.

"Lee."

"Come on, sweetheart. Nights like this are torture." Lee was at a point in his career where hitting these opening night spectacles was just about mandatory. Premieres were big game for the entertainment press, and Lee's name showing up in the next day's *Variety* kept him in the spotlight. But he hated the charade, and we were always the first to bolt when the lights came up at the end. We were pulling up to the theater, and I looked out of the darkened limo window.

"Uh-oh, Lee, Army's waiting." Army Archerd, top celebrity gossip columnist, rarely missed an opening night.

"Don't worry, I'll be on my best behavior," Lee said, knocking back his martini. Then he smiled at me. "Fun comes later," he murmured and gave me a soft kiss on the cheek.

Hoards of fans on the sidelines were shouting to celebrities gathered in front. Lee grabbed my hand before the limo door was opened.

"Okay, baby, let's get this over with," he said into my ear, and we entered the crowd.

Army pounced on us immediately. Lee went through his routine: yes, he was thrilled to be there; yes, we were having another baby; (when weren't we, this one made four) yes, he loved Elizabeth Taylor. My job during these moments was to stand there stock still and beam like a Stepford Wife. After years of practice, I had the frozen smile down.

Behind us, Charles and Lydia Heston were waiting to talk to Army. Lee found them boring at best, so he nodded silently and gave them the limelight. He took my elbow, nodding at Archerd, and got us out of there.

Floodlights scanned the crowd of film star royalty. Glancing around, I saw several trophy wives grabbing their moment to sparkle next to their celebrity husbands. They all had a studied look of Hollywood opulence—nervous money, a friend called it.

Lee and I mingled with the crowd, exchanging a number of greetings mixed with handshakes and fake kisses. Lee spotted Anne Bancroft coming toward us. He gave her a quick embrace, then put his arm around me. "Honey, meet Anne. She single-handedly got me through that wreck of a film in Mexico." Anne and I smiled at each other. *God, what great cheekbones,* I thought, *and intelligent eyes.* She didn't look at all like the many Bright Young Things who were all hair and no brains. I was disappointed that before we could talk she was swept back into the throng.

When the line formed to enter the theater, I realized that we were standing behind Joan Crawford, of all people, who was chatting with her date for the evening, an attractive young man whose eyes were glued to her. The perfect escort. I turned to Miss Crawford to speak, but she ignored me and looked directly at Lee, eyes sparkling.

"Well, Mr. Marvin, I've been wanting to meet you for a long time. I'm a big fan."

"Why, thank you, Miss Crawford. I believe you know Mrs. Marvin."

She still didn't acknowledge me. It was as though she'd never met her children's ex-nanny!" She was all eyes on Lee. "I have a project you might be interested in," she said. "There's a role that has your name all over it." She turned on her smile, all painted lips and white teeth. Of course she knew I was aware of her routine affairs with all her leading men.

Bitch.

"I'll be in touch," she said, and not a moment too soon we were ushered inside.

Cat on a Hot Tin Roof was, of course, terrific. It was hard to go wrong with Paul Newman and Elizabeth Taylor. I couldn't help wondering how Lee felt watching Newman's character, an alcoholic who was drunk for a lot of the movie.

As soon as the film was over Lee was ready to run over to Chez Jay, a favorite late-night spot of ours. The joint was packed, and a crowd was standing three deep waiting to get drunk, fed, or both. We were regulars, so Jay quickly found us a small table by the bar.

"Enjoy," he said as he left me to maneuver my pregnant belly into the small space between the table and chair. Lee greeted a few of his drinking buddies at the bar before joining me. The bartender sent over the usual double-dry Tanqueray martini for Lee and my usual Dubonnet and soda.

"Hey, Lee!" One of Lee's stuntman pals strolled over to our table with more drinks, making a comment about "the little lady" with "a duck in the oven." I winced and looked away. There seemed to be some commotion at the bar, but I wasn't really paying attention. I just wanted this jerk to move on and leave us alone. Then, suddenly, like a bolt out of the blue, there was a shout and a man from the end of the bar came flying through the air and crashed right into our table, taking our drinks with him. The onlookers at the bar were hooting, ready to enjoy what appeared to be the beginning of a brawl, but in no time Jay and his bouncers escorted the troublemakers out onto the street.

"I don't know why we come here on a Saturday night," I said.

"Because Jay has the best steaks in town," Lee said.

Jay sent over a bottle of his best champagne as an apology, and an hour later Lee had finished the champagne and was working on a bottle of cabernet. God, I was tired. I was seven months pregnant, had three kids at home, and it was going on midnight. There weren't a lot of nights Lee and I got to go out, and I missed our time alone together, but right then all I wanted to do was put my head down. In the middle of dinner, Lee abruptly put down his steak knife and looked at me long and hard.

"What's up, honey?" I asked. He suddenly seemed troubled.

"I have a confession to make." His eyes avoided mine. "I know I'm probably crazy for telling you this, but I don't want us to have any secrets." Then he downed his drink and dropped the bomb. "When I was in Mexico, I had an affair."

I froze, my eyes glued to my dinner plate.

"It didn't mean anything, sweetheart. *Gorilla at Large* was such a boring shoot. Anne and I—"

"Excuse me," I mumbled, getting out of the chair. After maneuvering my way through the mob to the ladies' room, I locked the door and leaned against it. *Gorilla at Large*. Anne . . . Anne Bancroft! Why did he have to tell me? What in hell was the deal introducing me to her a few hours ago? And why tell me now? I'm carrying his child, for God's sake. Son of a bitch! I could have killed him.

I felt trapped in my big, cumbersome body. I began to shake as I pictured Anne extending her hand to me. What if everyone already knew my husband had been cheating on me?

I stared into the mirror. I hardly recognized myself. Gone was the radiant "pregnant is beautiful" look. Instead, there appeared before me a bewildered, miserable creature. I leaned my head against the tile wall and bit my lip to keep from crying.

Half an hour must have passed before I finally returned to our table. Lee had finished his steak and was paying the bill.

I got through the next couple of months on automatic pilot, eager to reclaim my body. The afternoon before I was scheduled to go into the hospital to deliver our fourth child by cesarean, Lee and I went to a gathering in Malibu. Feeling nauseous from the tobacco smoke in the room, I waddled out onto the balcony, high above the rocks below, for a breath of fresh sea air.

A tall, blond, handsome man stood on the edge of the railing, smoking a cigarette and staring down as though he were about to jump.

"Are you sure you want to do that?" I called up to him.

He studied me carefully. "Why not? I don't know. Are you interesting?"

"Come down from there and find out."

He tossed his cigarette, jumped down, and came over to me. "Hello. I'm Tristram."

"What an unusual name."

"And that's only the beginning. I'm Tristram Coffin Colket the Third." He paused, then added, "M.D." I laughed as he sat down next to me.

"Are you with those people in there?" he asked.

"I'm with one of them."

"Shouldn't he or she be keeping an eye on you? From the looks of things, you're about to have a baby any minute."

I smiled. "Tomorrow morning. And, considering the circumstances, Doctor, I'm better off here with you."

We fell into a long conversation, ignoring the sunset.

As the sky turned dark, Lee came out. "Sorry to break this up, sweetheart, but we're due at the hospital."

I introduced him to Tris, my new friend. "I'll be there in a moment. Can you call Dr. Mishell and tell him we're on our way?" It was hard to tear myself away from this bright, funny, engaging man, and it was almost midnight by the time Lee and I reached the hospital.

Claudia Leslie was born the next morning, twenty-two months after Cynthia, at which time I opted for a tubal ligation. Lee was disappointed. He always was delighted with my pregnancies and very proud of each new addition. A few weeks after our last child was born, we were lying in bed after making love when he announced that sex with me would never be the same now that there was no chance of my getting pregnant. His remark made me sad. Was I just a baby machine to him?

I threw myself into mothering our children and tried to ignore my sadness. Not only did I have a newborn, I was a Camp Fire Girls Leader, a Cub Scout Den Mother and active in the PTA. I planned each child's birthday party as though it were a major event. No theme was ever repeated and our home was completely transformed for each holiday celebration. I had definitely bought into the family sitcoms of the fifties and was starring in "Mother Knows Best." Structure was everything as I became more and more of a "Dollhouse" wife. If I had the perfect family home, surely nothing could be wrong with my marriage.

The Perfect Family, Easter 1958

I found myself remembering the first few weeks with Lee. I was so happy in our first home together, that tiny furnished apartment. Now we lived in a six-thousand-square-foot house full of beautiful antiques, which brought me no happiness. The size and opulence of our home only added to my feelings of separation from my husband. More and more I looked forward to our times at Turtle Lodge, when we came together as a real family.

One evening Lee and I met Sharley and Keenan Wynn for dinner at La Scala, a fashionable Italian restaurant in Beverly Hills where the stars loved to hang out and hop from one leather booth to the next. Lee was deep in conversation with Keenan, but I was having a difficult time concentrating on what Sharley was saying, since, recently, when Lee and I were in New York, I had seen Keenan with some babe on his arm. At the time I had told Lee I didn't know if I could face Sharley after that.

"Why, Betty? It doesn't mean anything."

"Does Sharley know?"

"I doubt it."

"Then it's a clear case of deception."

"Come on, sweetheart. It's just a little lie."

"There's no such thing."

"Why do you have to make such an issue over this? It has nothing to do with you."

"Okay, let's forget it." But I couldn't, and here I was feeling guilty, for God's sake—as if I had committed a crime.

Jack Cassidy showed up at our table, obviously feeling no pain. "Lee, I want to tell you what a great actor you are. I love your work."

"Thanks, Jack." Lee went back to the point he was making to Keenan.

"I'm serious," Jack continued, oblivious. "You are the best. I love you."

"Well, thank you very much," Lee said, losing patience. He looked at us and rolled his eyes.

"I mean it," Jack persisted. "I love you."

Lee looked up, studied Jack, then rose from the table and gave him a full, wet kiss on the mouth. "Will that hold you for a while?"

Jack practically fell over from shock, but quickly regained his balance and silently staggered away.

After dinner Sharley and Keenan left, but Lee wanted to stay for a night cap. Over a brandy he cozied up to me.

"You know what I told you in Jay's?" he murmured.

I tensed. "I don't want to talk about it."

He stroked my neck. "Sweetheart, I need to tell you something. I don't know what came over me, confessing to such a thing. It never happened. I made it up. I didn't have an affair."

I looked at him in disbelief. Did he or didn't he? Which was worse—having an affair or lying about it?

15

Good Causes Raise Self Esteem

I was trying to hold it together, but our household was becoming increasingly tense. Lee's initial enthusiasm for *M Squad* was waning fast. He felt trapped in a role that was taking him nowhere, and his unhappiness began to take its toll. His behavior grew less rational. He'd come home drunk, or not come home at all. He was withdrawing more and more into himself, literally hiding from everyone.

Once, after he'd been missing for hours, I found him in his scuba gear, sitting at the bottom of the swimming pool.

"Talk to me, Lee," I asked him one night when I woke up and found him staring at the ceiling. "We need to fix this." He didn't respond. On the intercom I heard Claudia start to cry, and I got up and went down to her room.

When the Christmas season arrived, Anna, a beautiful, black, heavy-set woman, the widow of a Baptist minister, came to help me through the holidays and ended up staying. She made it possible for me to keep up the insane, backbreaking schedule I had created for my kids and myself with music lessons, dance, sports, charity, political and PTA meetings planned for every moment of the day. And with the tension in the house, it was a tremendous relief to have another adult there to help me. At first it felt strange having a woman older than myself with grown children of her own working for me. But her unwavering patience and kindness filled the house, and when I implored her to stay, she was happy to oblige. It was the first time she had worked since her husband's death.

One afternoon I came in after a PTA meeting and found Anna rocking five-year-old, thumb-sucking Courtenay instead of Claudia, who was napping. Anna was never too busy with her housework to stop everything and care for the children when I had to be away. Courtenay loved this special attention. Christopher and Cynthia came in from playing in the garden. Cynthia ran into my arms, but Christopher wanted some of Anna's special attention for himself. By the time he got to her, she already had an arm out for him; and as she held Courtenay with one arm, she gave Christopher a hug with the other.

"Some days I'd love to crawl onto your lap myself," I said, falling into a chair nearby.

"No, Mommy," Courtenay said. "Anna's mine."

"Mine," said Christopher.

Anna laughed. "Anna's here for anyone who needs her. I feel so blessed to have found you all."

"Anna, we're the ones who are blessed. I don't know how I ever managed without you. By the way, can you watch the kids tomorrow afternoon? I've made an appointment to have my hair done."

"Be happy to."

I had an appointment with Richard Alcala, the celebrity hairstylist of Beverly Hills. His salon was the hangout for Hollywood wives until he was busted for hiding pot in his vacuum cleaner. As Richard painted the perfect color into my hair, I heard the woman next to me say my name. "Betty Marvin?"

I turned and found an old friend who had just come in.

"Lois Clarke?"

She laughed. "Lois Garner, thank you."

"I know you and Jim are married now, but to me you're still Lois Clarke." When Lee and I were first married and he was away on location, Lois lived with me briefly before she became Mrs. James Garner. After her marriage our paths hadn't crossed until now.

"It's good to see you, Betty. I hear you have something like fifteen children."

"Not quite. But four can feel like fifteen sometimes."

"If you have time, call me. We must have dinner."

We exchanged numbers before I left the salon. During our conversation Lois mentioned she was a member of an organization called SHARE, a charity group made up of Hollywood wives. She thought I should join and gave me the group's phone number. I knew I needed to get out more, so I called SHARE and got the address of the next meeting.

"Never heard of them," Lee said when I told him about it. "But sure, go to the tea party or whatever."

"Damn it, Lee. I'm not interested in going to a tea party. I want to get involved with something meaningful."

"Don't you think being a wife and mother is meaningful?"

"I mean something out of the house."

"Honey, if it makes you happy, do it."

The meeting was being held in the Bel Air home of the wife of a well-known actor. I was duly impressed by the exterior, but the interior blew me away. It was all white on white. Before I got too far into the room, the hostess came up and greeted me by name; we'd met at industry functions before but didn't really know each other.

After a peck on each cheek, she smiled perkily and said, "Betty, dear, would you remove your shoes, please? The maid will take them for you." I was surprised, as this was long before Asian tradition had permeated our culture. Asking someone to take off his shoes when entering was about as common as asking someone to remove his shirt. But I did as I was told and sat on one of the white linen sofas, surrounded by a number of fashionable women. We were served a full tea, complete with cucumber sandwiches and cookies on a beautiful silver tray.

A tea party. Score one for Lee.

"Love your necklace," one woman said to another. "Did I see that at Winston's?"

"Oh, no. My husband had the stones cut and the piece designed for me."

Right. Surely we'd be getting to the charity work soon. I felt uncomfortable and reached for a cookie.

"God, did you see the dress she was wearing? She cannot wear Pucci, not with those hips." Bits of conversation wafting across the room reminded me of the sorority rush tea from college days, only now the girls were all grown women with even more money.

Finally the hostess took a central chair and began to talk about SHARE's next event.

"We've agreed that our next donation will go to the Children's Sponsorship Fund of Los Angeles." At last, the real reason we were there.

"I've written a check to Sy, and we'll have the Beverly Hills Playhouse in six weeks."

"Six weeks? How are we going to put on a show that quickly?" one woman asked. Everyone started talking at once.

"The costumes have to be custom."

"How will we have time to hire an orchestra?"

"I thought we agreed to do songs from *South Pacific* and *Oklahoma!* this year. The playhouse is all wrong for that show! We need a much bigger space!"

What the hell were they talking about? I reached for another cookie, dropping a few crumbs on the carpet as I picked it up. Without missing a beat, the hostess stood, went to the living room corner, and, smiling all the while, took hold of a brand-new, all-white, compact vacuum cleaner and propelled it toward me. "Excuse me!" she said quite perkily and vacuumed up the crumbs around my ankles.

"What's our show budget?"

Our hostess had returned to her throne and niftily returned the white vacuum cleaner to its ivory corner. "Well, we have nine thousand in the kitty for this show, but I know we can do better than that!"

Nine thousand dollars? This had nothing to do with the Children's Sponsorship Fund. This was a charity for fading showgirls who had married out of their careers and were willing to drop a ton of cash—their husbands' cash—to put on a vanity production.

Nobody noticed when I left. I had the maid retrieve my shoes and ran down the steps to my car.

"God! That was . . . horrible!" I exploded when I got home.

"All right, all right!" Lee was obviously tickled at my reaction. "So what does SHARE stand for, anyway?"

"I never found out. What about "Silly Hollywood Asses blah, blah . . ."

"You're too smart to hang out with those dames."

"Okay, but, Lee, I want to do something. I'm sick of being surrounded by people who have their heads in the sand."

Lee was in full agreement. Even though he was not political and only supported causes at my insistence, he respected my liberal beliefs. "What about Steve Allen and Robert Ryan's new organization?"

These Hollywood celebrities were just beginning to put together "Hollywood for SANE," born out of a New York group called Sane Nuclear Policy, headed by Norman Cousins. Our country was in the middle of the Cold War, and people were caught up in the idea of building bomb shelters on their property to protect themselves against a nuclear attack.

I joined Hollywood for SANE shortly after my one and only foray into SHARE, and before long I was hosting meetings in our home. They were a far cry from the charity event I'd attended in Bel Air. There was laughing, there was yelling, there was a lot of passion, and there were real plans hatched and executed. There was no compact vacuum.

After joining Hollywood for SANE, I became more and more active in politics. It was satisfying to be able to put time and money into causes I believed in and express my concerns with others who shared my beliefs. However, there were those good people who did not agree with my politics. I managed to remain friends with them in spite of our differences, although it wasn't easy in a time when fear penetrated our society.

"I want you all to know the race track is a thing of my past," Walter Matthau announced over dinner one night.

"Oh, come on, Walter," said Lee as he poured wine for our guests. "Playing the horses is your one great passion."

"Yeah, it was, but it cost me a fortune. Expensive habit. Hypnosis did it. I'm finished with the track."

"A toast to the end of vice," came a droll voice from the end of the table. Oscar Levant raised his glass with shaking hands—the result of too much drinking for too long—, and we all toasted Walter's being cured of gambling.

"I understand President Eisenhower had to go into the hospital for exploratory surgery," said our neighbor friend Dr. Robert Sinskey, the only Republican at the table.

"That's no surprise. They were probably looking for his spine," said Oscar, lighting a cigarette from the one flickering to an end in his stained fingers.

Everyone laughed but Robert, who most certainly hated Oscar's politics. Lee added fuel to the fire.

"Robert, tell us how your bomb shelter's coming along."

"Very well, thank you. As a doctor I have a responsibility to the community. I intend to use it to store medical supplies. I'm setting up a sort of first aid station in case of an attack."

"Isn't that kind of like putting a band aid on a hemorrhage? If there is an attack, wouldn't you be more concerned with getting your family into the shelter?"

"I'm sure I would."

Lee turned sinister. "Well, what if I told you I would take one of my guns, blow your head off, throw your family out, and take my family in?"

The table fell silent. Lee smiled and went over and patted Robert on the arm. "Just making a point, good neighbor."

Robert did not speak as the rest of the dinner guests eagerly returned to lighter conversation.

Rod Serling, the quiet listener at most parties, went home and wrote the bomb shelter conversation into an episode of *The Twilight Zone*.

Walter Matthau was spotted a few days later at the track.

16

Where Are You? Don't Tell Me

Working for political causes was satisfying, but I also needed to get my creative juices flowing again, and in that pursuit I discovered painting. I converted part of our four-car garage into a studio and began to study seriously with Keith Finch, one of Los Angeles's most successful abstract painters of the sixties. It was a perfect outlet because the kids could be in my studio and we would spend the afternoons making art together.

But when evening came, I became lonelier and lonelier. *M Squad* was an all-encompassing show. Not only were the hours long, but Lee had fallen into the habit of stopping after the day's shooting for a few drinks with the grips before coming home. He was more and more unavailable.

At first I protested with anger and tears, but my complaints were met with excuses and apologies. At last I realized nothing I said made any difference. Lee had become addicted to the adulation . . . and to the booze. It had reached the point where I never knew when or if he would come home or in what condition. I'd check in with him during the day to see how late he would be. After the children went to bed, I would fix his dinner, then listen to music, read, or watch television and wait. And wait. Many nights his dinner would go from the oven and eventually into the garbage disposal, and I would go to bed enraged.

That's when the real torture began. By now I knew Lee would be drunk and racing his Arnolt Bristol sports car around the sharp curves of Sunset Boulevard. I would lie there hour after hour, night after night, listening for his car to pull into the garage, hating him for coming home late but scared that one night he wouldn't make it home at all. A couple of fatal accidents had already occurred on those curves.

As Lee's misery with the TV series grew deeper, my concern for his welfare was so great that I rented an apartment for him across the street from the studio, furnished it with his personal necessities, and begged him to stay there after work. The first night in his new temporary residence he called.

"Oh, baby, please let me come home," he begged. "I need you. Please let me come home. I don't want to sleep in this dump. Why are you punishing me? I love you."

"I love you too. That's why I don't want you driving. You're in no shape to drive."

"Then come get me. Don't leave me here alone. I need you."

And so I got out of bed, asked Anna to keep an ear out for the children, and went to his rescue. "How crazy can I get?" I asked myself on the forty-minute drive to Studio City. But from an early age, I had been taught that being needed was the same as being loved.

One evening Lee was missing again, and dear friend Tris came around to keep me company. I poured myself a glass of wine and gin on the rocks for Tris. "God, it's good to see you," I said, "I love my kids to pieces, but at night I'm dying for some adult company."

"And I, on the other hand, have been with boring adults all day and want to play with the kids," Tris said. "Where are they?"

"Asleep, long ago."

"Damn, I missed them." He picked up his drink. "Let's go out into the courtyard. I want to show you something."

"Okay," I said, "but first let me show you something." We walked into my art studio, a line Lee never crossed. My husband was completely oblivious to my painting. Tris, on the other hand, was always eager to see my work. I handed him my latest pen-and-ink drawing. He studied it for some time.

"This is so much like Munch, with that long, lonely line. What were you looking at when you drew this?"

"I did it with my eyes closed. I see better that way."

We left the studio and walked out into the cool night air.

"Ready?" Tris said, turning to me. He rolled up his sleeve and reached into his jacket pocket, pulled out a syringe kit, prepared a needle, put a tourniquet on his arm, and quickly gave himself an injection. Then he sat down on a garden chair and rolled up his pants. "Now watch the drug travel down the veins of my leg," he said matter-of-factly as he traced the pathway with a marker.

"Oh, what a feeling," he murmured as the drug took effect. I'd seen Tris shoot up before. He always explained his addiction to prescription drugs as medical research, continually performing experiments upon his own body and freely prescribing drugs for his own consumption. "All for the sake of science," he smiled up at me faintly. I had no idea what drugs he was using.

Tris and I had a deep connection. We fueled each other's curiosity and found release in deep conversations. We were also bonded by the arts. He was a great jazz pianist and I loved to sing. As with Jerry Rogers in the past, I had a friend teaching me songs I'd never heard before. So, that night we spent the next few hours at the piano. Sitting next to him, I felt a strong attraction. But even if I were to consider an affair, which I didn't, there was no possibility of it ever happening. Nothing would come between him and his drugs. He had his mistress.

After Tris left, Lee called and engaged in his "guess where I am" routine, a game he loved to play with me when he was drunk. I was furious. After he hung up I called the bars and asked for him but got the usual reply: "He's not here" or, "He just left." Bartenders are such liars.

Finally, I'd had it. Spinning out of control, I got the children out of bed and piled them into the back seat of the station wagon. (It was Anna's day off.) I raced from bar to bar trying to find Lee. Seeing his car in the parking lot of a bar near the studio, I went inside. He wasn't there. I looked inside his car and found a woman's rhinestone hair combs on the seat. This was more information than I needed. I drove home, hiding tears from the kids and realizing then I didn't want to know what he did on his nights out.

I never went looking for Lee again. But bad news came looking for me. One night of waiting I received a phone call from a drunk Rosemary Clooney, asking for our address so she could have Lee delivered to our home. Another time the Los Angeles health department came to the front door with a notice that a prostitute had namedLee as a possible venereal disease recipient. I was relieved when his test for the disease was negative.

Slowly things were going from bad to worse.

17

Hitting the Bottom Blues

My thirtieth birthday was approaching, and Robert Walker wanted to give me a party. He sent out invitations to forty of my close friends for a black-tie, sit-down dinner in his beautiful courtyard. I knew he was going to great pains to make everything just right. He had asked to have my recipe for veal scaloppine and had hired Greta, a talented German chanteuse, to sing my favorite songs.

That morning of July 16, 1958, Lee gave me a bicycle with a diamond watch in the basket. I should have been happy to have such a generous husband and excited to be going to a special, elegant party given just for me, but I was so depressed I could hardly make it through the day. To make matters worse, I had no one to confide in. That afternoon I went into the garden and walked and walked through the acre of flower beds I had planted that spring. Even the beauty of the endless blooms did not cheer me. Tris arrived unexpectedly, throwing me a lifeline.

"What are you doing here?" I said, grateful he'd come.

I hung on to his embrace. He finally pulled back and looked at me with concern. "What's the matter, baby? What's going on?" He took my hand and we continued to walk.

"I don't know. I dread this party tonight. I'm afraid to leave my house. I don't want to see anyone. I feel guilty, but I wish I could get out of it."

"Well, you can't."

"What's happening to me, Doctor?"

"I'd say you're having a bit of an anxiety attack coupled with deep-seated depression. Both conditions are my constant companions. I know them well."

"How can you stand it?"

"I can't. Thank God for chemical assistance—though I know you don't approve."

"Tris, I have a husband, four young children, and a house to run. I can't get into drugs."

"I know, but let me give you a valium. Just one. Take a long, hot shower, then lie down until the party. What time will Lee be home?"

"Your guess is as good as mine."

"It's your birthday. I'm sure he'll be here to take you to the party."

"Don't count on it."

"Call me if you need an escort."

Tris waited while I showered, gave me a pill, and tucked me in for a much-needed nap. Lee came home sober and on time. He was loving and attentive the whole evening, and I made it through the party with the added love of friends.

My thirtieth birthday, July 16, 1958

From that day on I felt myself slowly slipping into a black hole. As fall moved toward the holidays, I threw myself into the usual traditional activities, but it took all my energy to make it from one Hollywood party to the next, including a black-tie Christmas soiree thrown by Anne and Kirk Douglas.

"Could this be an early evening?" I asked Lee as we were getting ready to go.

"Where's your party spirit, sweetheart? A glass of champagne will pick you up."

"I don't feel like driving home tonight. Try not to drink so much."

"Don't worry about it. I'll be fine."

"Merry Christmas, Betty," said my charming hostess, Anne. "You look fabulous."

"I feel fabulous," I lied, forcing a laugh, as I, covered in mink, made my way into the barroom. Little did she know I was hanging on to the barstool to keep from keeling over. I dreaded the dinner hour because I could barely open my mouth to eat in front of anyone.

Lee had abandoned me at the front door and was already entertaining the guests, so I was on my own. *Just get through this. Don't tell anyone anything. Just perform,* I pleaded with myself all through the party. That morning I had been shocked to realize, when pulling the carpool station wagon into our garage, that I had forgotten my daughter Claudia at Hughes market.

Oh, my God, what kind of a mother am I? I can't be trusted with my own kid. My husband never comes home at night, and why should he? I'm a mess, a failure as a wife and as a mother. What's happening to me?

Is this what it's like to go crazy, I wondered. Ever since working at the Washington State Mental Hospital as a teenager, I'd had a tremendous fear of going crazy. Was it happening? I had begun to lock myself in the bathroom at night in case I got out of control. I was desperate. All I wanted was to give up the charade, check into Cedars, and get on with a nice, civilized breakdown.

Instead, I went into analysis.

Five mornings a week, at precisely 11:00 AM, I crawled to my analyst feeling very shabby in my mink. I drove the most elegant, white Continental convertible up "Libido Lane" to that well-known Analysts' Building on Bedford in Beverly Hills, loaded with famous, successful shrinks. I recognized other patients in the elevator, but I never saw their eyes behind their dark glasses. We never spoke.

What I really thought about when wearing my first mink coat was that my devoutly unfaithful husband must have really screwed up to feel guilty enough to buy it in the first place. His crime had to be greater than the one that produced the three-carat diamond ring, the fourth of five wedding rings presented to me in eight years. Why the sham of constantly asking me to be his wife when we were already married and he obviously had no respect for the institution?

But this one purchase, after he had been particularly neglectful, included the ritual of selecting the pelts, choosing the style, and enduring endless fittings. Everything was custom. Some custom. Secretly, I found the wearing of dead animals offensive, but then I, too, was dead in a way and felt nothing, except undeserving. Lee, however, felt good every time I wore the fur. And making him feel good was part of my job. After all, I was responsible for his happiness, wasn't I?

"How does your husband feel about your coming here for treatment?" Dr. Rangell's gentle voice and quiet manner were encouraging. He studied me with his kind eyes, waiting for my response. I still felt shy and self-conscious though I'd been in analysis for several weeks.

"I haven't seen him lately to ask."

"Oh, is he away?"

"No. He comes home after I've gone to bed. Sometimes he just doesn't come home."

"Without telling you?"

"Well, he's very busy when he's working, and sometimes he can't get home."

"Where does he stay?"

"I don't know." This exchange was making me very uncomfortable.

"Is he this wonderful husband you've been telling me about?" he asked.

I began to cry. "When I first told him I wanted to go into analysis, he said if I did it would be the end of our marriage."

"Why do you think he's against it?"

"I guess he doesn't want things to change. I don't know what to do. I know I need help, but I'm afraid I'll lose my marriage. I can't afford that. He needs me to take care of him. He would never even make it to work if I didn't get him up."

"Is that your job? Don't you have enough to do taking care of the children? Don't you have an alarm clock?"

"Yes, but if he's stays out drinking he'll never set it. Even if I set it, he'll never hear it. If I don't get him up, he'll miss his call at the studio, and—"

"Is that your problem?" Dr. Rangell would not let me off the hook. My time was up. He smiled reassuringly as he closed the door behind me.

As usual, Lee was out late that night. I set his alarm and was asleep when he came home. The next morning when it was time for his alarm to go off, I was fixing breakfast for the children. I could not hear the alarm, but I began to tremble. It took all my strength to resist going upstairs to awaken him. An hour later the phone rang.

"For God's sake, Betty, where is he?" It was Joe in the makeup department at the studio.

"He's asleep."

"Oh, no!" Joe said and hung up.

Then someone from MCA called.

"We just heard from the studio. Where is he?"

"He's asleep."

"Well, we'll stall them. Just tell him to get his ass to work." The man hung up, and reluctantly I went upstairs.

"Lee." I shook the stretched-out, snoring body, mostly hidden by covers. "Lee, wake up." I patted his cheek.

"Uhmmm," he moaned.

"Better get up. Both the studio and MCA have called. You've overslept." I stepped back.

"What?" He shot out of bed. "What happened? Why the fuck didn't you call me?"

I took a deep breath. "I was downstairs feeding the kids." I gulped, took another breath, and added, "Your alarm went off." Then summoning all my courage, I added, "It's not my job to get you up. I'm not your mother." I thought I was going to faint as I made my way back to the kitchen. When the fear finally subsided, I felt good.

A few minutes later Lee came storming through the kitchen where the kids were eating.

"What's gotten into you? Is this your analysis talking?" I had no time to answer as he ranted on. "Well, I'll tell you one thing. If you keep this up you can kiss your marriage good-bye." I remained calm in the eye of the storm as he slammed the door and was gone.

I turned to the kids, pretending to be all right. "More pancakes, anyone?"

18

Paris V Brings High Fashion at a Low Time

During this painful time, something completely unexpected happened. I was at a cocktail party given by a good friend, fashion designer Rudi Gernreich. He was introducing his line of rather shocking black knit bathing suits, and early in the evening he asked me to model one for the guests. I ducked into his bedroom and put the thing on, but I couldn't imagine what he was thinking.

"Come on, Rudi, I look like my grandfather in this," I said, posing in the skimpy, tight suit with holes the size of silver dollars. The reflection in the mirror of my small breasts, narrow hips, and long, thin legs was confirmation.

"Wrong," said Rudi definitively. "You have the body this suit was made for."

"You've got to be joking!" But he wasn't.

"Maybe I should give you the topless one to wear!"

"Not on your life," I told him. "But, okay, just for this evening I'll model."

Rudi loved me in his clothes, and I was with him in New York when he showed his collection at the Algonquin Hotel, a place that was home to Lee and myself when we were in New York.

Lee also loved the way I looked in Rudi's clothes. He thought I had great style.

One evening he told me he'd seen me on Wilshire Boulevard. "You looked so damned good. I thought, *What a beautiful woman. I've got to check her out.* I drove up along side the car and there you were—my own wife!"

Spending time with Rudi was fun and brought interesting people into my life, including Avis Caminez, an international fashion consultant. When he suggested I accompany him on his next trip to Paris, I surprised myself by saying yes. A few months earlier I never would have considered it. I knew the kids would be fine if I left them with Anna for a couple of weeks, and I needed a holiday from Lee.

Rudi was eager to market his collection in Paris and convinced me I could act as his representative while there. He set up meetings with the five top designers, including Dior and Lanvin.

Before I mentioned my travel plans to my husband, I consulted Dr. Rangell. His response was so positive he almost pushed me out the door and onto a plane. Lee was agreeable, so a few weeks later I set off for two weeks on my first trip to Europe. I had always hoped it would be with Lee, but I had grown tired of waiting for him to take a real holiday.

From the time I checked into the fashionable Hôtel de Crillon and walked up Rue de Rivoli in my ocelot coat and Russian sable hat toward the Arc de Triomphe, I felt as if I'd come home.

My life as a full-time mother and wife seemed, for those short weeks, far away as I entered the world of Paris fashion. The designers Rudi had arranged for me to meet not only loved his work but also had ambitions of their own: they wanted their high-end designs on the backs of fashionable, well-to-do women in the United States. By my fourth day in Paris, I was already starting to discuss how I might represent them in Los Angeles. By the time I was flying home, with Avis's guidance, I'd made agreements to represent many of the best names in the fashion industry. It had happened so quickly I could scarcely believe it.

"I'm glad you're home." Lee was planting kisses all over my face. "I missed you."

"I missed you too," I murmured, thinking if only I'd known this would be the result, I would have gone on a trip ages ago.

Lying in bed later that night, I told Lee about the deals I'd made in Paris. He seemed impressed, and when I got up my nerve and said I'd need $10,000 to open a boutique, he said, "Okay. I'll call Ed in the morning." That was it.

Ed Silver, our long-time financial adviser, knew better than to argue with Lee when he said, "Betty wants it, that's why." But when Ed gave me the money to start the business, he said, "Hope this investment is a loss so we can write it off."

I scouted for the right property in the right location and soon established Paris V, the first boutique on Rodeo Drive in Beverly Hills representing Christian Dior, Lanvin, Guy Laroche, Jacques Heim, and Jean Dessès. I had my own business, and I loved it.

Paris V, 1960

At first Lee loved it too. He was relieved for me to have a challenging project since he was away most of the time. *M Squad* was rolling on, and however unhappily, he was still attached.

In short order Paris V was booming, and I hired a manager so I would not be away from the children when they were home. The boutique was open by appointment only. To add to the collection of imports, I ordered custom furs and hats that were made in Beverly Hills but designed by well-known names in French fashion. The Beverly Hills Hotel gave me its antique jewelry on consignment for the European models to wear. I arranged to introduce the collections at the Brown Derby Restaurant in Beverly Hills on the same day they were being shown in Paris. When Lanvin came out with a new perfume, I held a high tea fashion show and invited all my best customers, providing each with a gift of the new scent.

At another event, I pulled in Lee as emcee. We had a blast that evening as he introduced the models, who ran in their finery from Paris V, across the alley, and through the kitchen of the Brown Derby restaurant before finally landing in the dining room. They paraded among the seated guests, flashing antique jewelry, seductively dropping their furs, and removing their hats at the appropriate moment to reveal the latest Parisian design. A live combo played jazz in the background. It was a high-fashion striptease, and the audience loved it. As usually happened, that night we sold the complete collection right off the floor.

Paris V was such a big success we had the best-dressed women in the country as clients. I still never really cared about shopping or fashion per se, usually grabbing something from the collection at the last minute to wear for the show. But this business was like theater. It was great fun, at least for a couple of years.

Lee, Tris, and I with the "best-dressed" clients at a Paris V gala

When the drinking got so bad he couldn't avoid facing it anymore, Lee admitted he needed to get some help. He made several attempts at Alcoholics Anonymous. Unfortunately, he usually stopped for a couple of martinis on his way to meetings, claiming it was the only way he could get through those evenings. He finally gave up. "The whole sad lot of them are nothing but a bunch of frustrated actors," he declared. "They can hardly wait for their turn to get onstage and tell the rest of us drunks the boring story of their miserable lives."

Finally, Lee told me he was going on suspension rather than do *M Squad* for another season. He was deeply depressed and started drinking at home during the day. He said he needed me to be with him. The decision was easy. I sold the inventory, canceled my lease, and closed Paris V.

Out of desperation, Lee went to Meyer, his old agent, and begged for him to take him back. Meyer negotiated with MCA and made a deal to again represent Lee.

"Guess what? I'm getting married." I almost fell over when Tris delivered the news to me during a casual phone call. "I would love to have the wedding at your house. What do you say?"

What could I say? My dear friend was tying the knot! "Fine. When?"

"You don't sound very enthused?"

"I'm just surprised. Who's the lucky lady?"

"Kay. I'll bring her over tonight. She's American Indian. I call her 'Black Cloud.'"

"That sounds promising."

"She's strange but beautiful. You'll love her."

That night I met Kay, an attractive brunette with ice-blue eyes that were out of focus. It appeared Tris had met a drug partner.

Two weeks later I gave them a wedding. Lee was the best man; I, the maid of honor. The evening of the big event, Kay, while changing into her wedding suit in our master bedroom, got high on pot. She swayed down the stairs behind our daughters, who were the flower girls. Claudia, three, was in tears as she picked up the rose petals being tossed by Cynthia and Courtenay.

"You're dropping your fowers!" she cried out.

At the last minute Tris had engaged the services of a senile minister who kept repeating himself and losing his place in the scriptures, while Kay, leaning on Tris, laughed and delivered constant *amens*. Our small wedding party found the whole thing entertaining, and we ended the evening with a lavish dinner party at the Beverly Hills Hotel.

A few weeks later Tris sent Black Cloud to stay with us while he moved to Livermore to work at the Rand Research Lab, developing questions for which there were already answers. His brilliant, abstract mind was perfect for that complex task but could not handle the simple ground rules for marriage.

The divorce took place shortly after the wedding, and Tris took a year off from medicine and went around the world playing jazz piano.

19

Lee's Affair with the Bottle: Losing Hope

When Lee was cast in *Donovan's Reef*, the studio rented a big, airy beach house for our family in a coconut plantation on the island of Kauai, and we all sailed on the Matsonia to Hawaii for the summer.

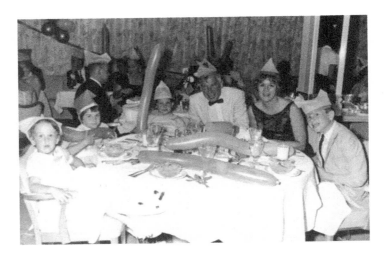

Sailing with the family to Hawaii in 1962

The first evening at sea, John Wayne spotted us and came over to our dinner table to greet Lee. They hadn't seen each other since *The Man Who Shot Liberty Valance; their* reunion was loud and warm.

"Duke, meet my family," Lee said proudly, turning to our table. "My wife, Betty, my daughters, Claudia, Courtenay, and Cynthia, and my son, Christopher."

I gave him my best smile and a warm hello, and the girls managed polite greetings, but Christopher just glared at Duke, refusing his big, outstretched hand. I was embarrassed by my son's rudeness, but later Christopher exclaimed, "I hate that man! He shot my dad!" He had remembered Wayne from *The Man Who Shot Liberty Valance*. But Duke won him over at breakfast the next day.

"Hey, pal, ever see a horse race?" Christopher balefully shook his head.

"C'mon with me. I'll show you how to pick a horse and bet on him. Hope you don't mind," he added, turning to me with an endearing smile. "It's something every man needs to know."

By the end of the sea journey, Christopher had happily become Duke's runner, placing bets and gathering tips. My daddy would have been proud.

Kauai was beautiful, and we moved with ease into a relaxed tropical summer—swimming, sunning, and dining on fish and fruit. Though he was shooting during the week, Lee spent all his spare time romancing me and playing with the kids.

On the beach in Kauai

We also played a lot with other members of the cast: Jack Warden, Elizabeth Allen, but especially with Duke and his wife, Pilar. Next to the giant presence of her husband, Pilar, a lovely petite woman, practically disappeared. They were an odd couple, a big, lumbering, all-American guy and this tiny, elegant Spanish beauty. I hated Duke's politics but fell in love with his teddy bear charm.

A familiar face showed up at the one local saloon on our first night out—Cesar Romero, another cast member. When we spotted each other he did a double take. "Missy?" he asked with a curious look on his face. He hadn't seen me since Crawford's.

"Betty Marvin," I laughed. "I'm here with my husband and our kids."

"What a nice surprise," Cesar said, pulling me to my feet. "Come and dance with me."

"It's so good to see you," he said as he swept me around the floor. "You look absolutely wonderful. And I see I've found a dancing partner on this island."

"Hula!" a loud voice announced over the P.A. system. "Five minutes till the hula contest!"

The mai tais had me feeling good, so I jumped at the chance. "Come on, everyone," I clapped my hands at our table. "Hula time!"

Pilar and Elizabeth were quickly up on their feet, but Lee, Jack, and Duke held tight. "You're not getting me up there wiggling around," Jack announced.

The tourists' favorite *Hookelau* started to play, and almost everyone in the bar was on the floor in formation acting out the lyrics. I managed to get Lee up, and eventually Jack was pressed into service by Elizabeth, but Duke held fast, simply shaking his head no.

Doing the hula with John Wayne seemed too great an experience to pass up. "Come on, big guy," I insisted. "We're going to a hookelau." He practically fell to the floor laughing as we threw our nets out into the sea.

On my birthday Duke and Pilar gave me a little dinner party. Duke and Lee broke out a bottle of bourbon and got into shop talk. "Oh, come on, Lee, you know I'm no actor!" Duke stood up, laughing. "I've got this walk"—he began to imitate his infamous amble—"and I've got this talk"—he continued in that John Wayne growl—"but that's it!"

As Lee and I were getting ready to make our exit, Duke disappeared for a moment. He returned carrying a brown paper bag, which he offered me with his head half-down. "Happy birthday," he mumbled shyly. "Sorry for the wrapping." In the bag was an Hawaiian mumu he had chosen himself. When he saw how pleased I was, he blushed.

When the shoot was over, the company and their families were invited to spend the weekend in Oahu before flying home together. The children and I flew ahead and waited for Lee to join us. When he did not show up at the hotel, I called the location manager. He said Lee had been drinking but had boarded the plane with the rest of the cast for the short island hop. I tried to remain calm while the island police conducted a secret search.

Three days later I received word from our neighbor at home that he had found Lee passed out in our garden. In an alcoholic haze, he had flown back to Los Angeles alone looking for us, believing we were home. The children and I flew back with the cast and crew, who were all extremely kind to us, knowing the sad truth of the situation. When we arrived home Lee was pacing back and forth in the playroom. I sent the children in to see Anna and went to him. He could barely make eye contact.

"I'm a hopeless alcoholic," he said finally. "Please help me."

I called Dr. Mishell, who he got Lee into a detox center.

"You can do this," I told him before he entered the center, holding him tight.

"I'm scared," he whispered.

"I know, Lee, but I'm here, and I'm telling you, you can do this. You're the strongest man I've ever known."

"So here goes nothing." He gave me a weak smile, we kissed, and I watched him walk up the path into an old Victorian house in the bowels of Los Angeles. It felt so strange driving away, leaving him in those tacky surroundings, more uncertain of what the outcome of his stay would be than I wanted to admit.

Weeks later, back home, Lee went back to AA meetings determined to stay sober. He even asked Dr. Rangell to recommend an analyst for him. "Don't give it too much hope," Dr. Rangell told me. "Analysis rarely works for alcoholics. But it's worth a try."

Lee went to his analyst at UCLA five days a week, and I felt more hopeful now that we were both in treatment. He really tried. He counted the weeks, days, minutes, and seconds between drinks. I counted with him, praying he would be able to stay sober. Sadly, the periods of sobriety were accompanied by terrible depression. I could always tell when he was going to fall off the wagon because he would become very cheerful and affectionate. I loved him this way but knew what lay ahead. I joined Al-Anon to be supportive, feeling my behavior played a role in his sobriety.

One day Lee answered the phone. When he hung up, his face was ashen.

"My mother's dead." No more words passed between us, but I felt a twinge of guilt for the lack of love between my mother-in-law, Courtenay, and myself. We left the children with Anna and caught the first flight to New York. When the attendant came by to take drink orders before we took off, Lee ordered a double Tanqueray martini, very dry, with a twist. I looked at him, showing my disappointment.

"Don't worry, sweetheart. I'm fine. And you know what? Now that the wicked witch is dead, I don't need analysis anymore."

I realized then nothing had changed. Nothing was going to change. Wishing would not make it so.

The whole week in Woodstock neither Lee, his brother, Robert, nor his father, Lamont, drew a sober breath. At the service a drunken Lee threw himself on the casket, sobbing uncontrollably, "Mommy, don't leave me. Don't leave me."

It made me sad to see him this way, perhaps because I realized the pity I felt for him was killing my love. He drank steadily and quietly on the way home, speaking little, gone from the world.

Despite Lee's continuing battle with alcohol, he was still getting roles in major features. The summer of 1964 he was signed to play an ex-baseball star in Stanley Kramer's *Ship of Fools*. It was a plum role for him in a cast that included Simone Signoret, Vivien Leigh, Elizabeth Ashley, and José Ferrer. We rented a summer beach house, as was our custom, in Malibu. Vivien Leigh took a place a few houses away. Her houseguest for the summer was Sir John Gielgud, who spent most of the time indoors. I think he was allergic to the sun. Simone Signoret was our houseguest, sharing the guest quarters with our new friend Larry Hagman, a young actor from New York. Larry had come to Hollywood without his wife and two children looking for work. Lee and I met him at a party and found him very engaging, and he was in our lives from that moment on. He was lonely for his family, so he moved in almost immediately and became a welcome part of ours.

Lee and I had had a lot of people come and stay with us, mostly struggling actors. But Larry was different. Being Mary Martin's son and having performed in theater, he wasn't the typical young, starstruck actor. He, like Lee, had pizzazz, commanded attention, was larger than life. And Larry had amazing confidence—no job when he moved into our guest quarters, but amazing confidence.

Vivien Leigh was a beautiful, aging, blond coquette, typecast in the film, but in many ways quite different in person. I found her self-indulgent, her rather vulgar behavior fascinating. She had a fetish for costume jewelry, which she carried in her handbag and changed with each activity. One afternoon I suggested we take a swim. "Marvelous," she said. She quickly removed her beach baubles and put on an array of fish pins. The afternoon we attended the 1964 Summer Olympics in downtown Los Angeles, she was adorned in beads, bangles, and earrings with sports motifs. She admired my beach bag with shells so much that I gave her one as a birthday gift. From that day on the bag went with her everywhere, no matter what the occasion. One evening it even accessorized a black silk cocktail dress.

One day at the studio she and I were having lunch in her dressing room. When her mail was delivered, she examined a letter from her ex-husband, Sir Laurence Olivier, who still carried a torch for her. "Oh, poor Larry," she said dismissively as she opened the envelope. She read the contents quickly and threw them on the floor where they stayed. She turned back to me. "Now where were we?"

I continued to spend time with Vivien, who amused me, although it was Simone Signoret who really fascinated me. Vivien and Simone disliked each other. They were so different. Simone was perfectly cast in the movie as a political activist. I liked her politics and I liked her. She was beautiful, intelligent, and sophisticated.

During the filming of *Ship of Fools*, our home was the gathering place for the cast and their friends. In spite of my eroding marriage, I entertained nonstop—endless brunch, lunch, and dinner parties, followed by late nights around the piano. Lee's drinking obviously went way beyond the others'. He drank all the time and rarely ate with the rest of us. It became impossible to ignore his losing battle with booze.

One hot Sunday afternoon, I watched him crawling up the beach clutching a bottle of vodka. I was heartsick, knowing the children would see their father in this condition. But I could not always protect them, and

I no longer had the strength to nurse him or my fantasy that he was going to change. Finally, I learned to ignore him drunk. So did the children and our friends.

As I got to know Simone, my respect for her grew. She was a smart woman and seemed to have great insight into men and how to treat them. I liked the way she had dealt with her husband Yves Montand's brief affair with Marilyn Monroe during the filming of *Let's Make Love*. Without a word she flew back to Paris and went incommunicado. I was impressed that she, in her French fashion, could remain detached from his various dalliances during their marriage. Unfortunately, I could not detach myself from Lee's unfaithfulness.

Simone had become very fond of Lee and was saddened by his obvious spiral downward. She also saw the trouble I was in with my marriage. One day she had a driver take her into town and returned with a book for me, leaving it on my bed. It was a copy of Malcolm Lawry's *Under the Volcano*, the story of a hopeless alcoholic.

Later in the day I started reading; I got through the first few chapters and collapsed. I could not stop sobbing. It was impossible to ignore the heartbreaking message beiong sent me through Lawry's writing. I did not come out of my room at the usual cocktail hour in order to keep the children and our houseguests from seeing me with, swollen eyes. Lee was staying in town that night rather than making the long commute to the beach, so I feigned a headache and instructed Anna to feed the kids and deliver my apologies to all. I hid under the comforter, curled up in a fetal position, and fell asleep. Later in the evening Simone came to check on me.

"Betty, may I come in?"

I sat up in bed and turned on the side table lamp. "I'm embarrassed for you to see me like this."

She came over, gave me a tender embrace, and sat down next to me. She spotted the open book on my bed. "I'm sorry my gift has upset you. As a friend, I wanted to send you a message, but I'm afraid I've just made things worse. Please forgive me. You have enough pain."

"No, I have to face the truth. I just wish my problems were fiction, like in the novel."

"To watch you suffering breaks my heart. You put up such a brave front." She paused as I dried my tears. "You know, dear Betty, Lee isn't going to change. How long do you think you can go on like this?"

"I have to hang on. Maybe he'll go back to AA. We have four children. I can't raise them alone.

"What do you think you are doing now?"

"I know. But at least we're a family. I came from a divorce. I promised myself I would never let that happen to my children."

"Do you think it's good for them to see him like this?"

I fell silent. Then I shook my head and sighed. "Even if I had the courage to raise the kids alone, I can't leave Lee. He needs me. What would he do?"

"Lee will always have someone to take care of him. Fame's like that. Some people will do anything to be near it. Like moths to the flame."

"I feel sorry for them."

"Don't. It's time you think of yourself. You have four kids to raise." Her words brought more tears and she held me tight. "I've said too much."

"No. You're telling me what I already know. It's just that hearing the words makes it seem so damn real." I tried a smile. "Believe it or not, I'll get through this."

"Of course you will." Simone stood up and kissed me on both cheeks. "Try to get some sleep. I'll see you at breakfast." She gently closed the door behind her, and I crawled back under the covers.

20

Lee's Other Affair: Losing Heart

The night of the *Ship of Fools* wrap party at Chasen's, David, an old friend from Sedro-Woolley High, was in town for a dental convention. I invited him to come along. That day I gave myself the expensive gift of a makeover at Aida Grey in Beverly Hills. After the body and facial massage with exotic oils and creams and then a completely new makeup, including V-shaped, heavy black lines to extend the eyelids for an oriental effect, I returned home with my new face and a bag full of the makeover magic. I marched into

Lee's study.

"What do you think?" I asked, giving him a good look.

"About what, sweetheart?" he answered, barely looking up from his script.

"About me," I said, putting my face close enough to force his attention. "Don't you see anything different?" He took a good look.

"Oh, you've changed your hair."

"I haven't changed my hair, and I'm not going to change my hair until Sassoon tells me to change my hair. You're hopeless," I said, exasperated.

"I don't know what to say, honey. You always look great. You know I don't care how you look."

"Well, you'll be glad to know I just wasted a day and a fortune at Aida Grey."

"Spend as much as you want," he said, going back to his reading.

I turned on my heel and muttered, "Thanks."

A few hours later David came by the house. Many years had passed, but his appearance was pretty much the same. Of course he was older, had put on a few pounds, and had lost some of his hair. He seemed impressed when I led him through the formal living room into the paneled playroom. I went to the bar and fixed us each a drink. Lifting my martini glass to his tumbler of scotch and water, I made a toast. "Here's to us." The four children ran in and I introduced them. They noticed my new look immediately. Christopher stared at my face. "What happened to your eyes?"

"Mommy's playing dress up," Courtenay said.

"You look funny, Mommy," Cynthia chirped.

Claudia giggled. "Funny Mommy."

They all laughed. Anna came in and took the hecklers away.

David took it all in. "Four kids. I can't believe it."

"Neither can I. What a relief not to be pregnant," I sighed. "How long has it been since we've seen each other?"

"Fifteen years."

"No, it can't be," I said. "I'm so glad you called. Bring me up to date. Tell me everything."

"Well, there's not much to tell. I get up, go to the office, fill teeth, and come home. My life's pretty boring compared to yours."

"Weren't you engaged to . . . what's her name?"

David laughed. "Maureen."

"What happened to her?"

"I married her. We had three kids and got divorced."

We sat silent, secretly studying each other. He was the same sweet David. "I used to have the biggest crush on you," I confessed. He lit my cigarette.

"I never knew it. Probably just as well. This is a far cry from Sedro-Woolley. You know, Betty, you've really got it all."

I heard Lee's car. Crossing through the courtyard, he saw me through the window and called out as he came in the door. "Honey, did you pick up my clothes at the cleaners? My flight leaves first thing in the morning." He spotted David.

"Darling, this is my friend David," I said.

"David the dentist," he said warmly, extending his hand. "Am I ever glad to see you." He opened his mouth and pointed. "I had a root canal over four weeks ago. It still hurts. Why is that? Do you think he did the wrong tooth?" Before David could answer Lee looked at his watch. "Jesus, we've got to get going. The wrap party is starting. David, you'll join us."

When we arrived at Chasen's, the fashionable restaurant was packed with the rich and famous. David and I sat in a red leather booth while Lee mingled. David was awestruck and almost fainted when Simone Signoret came over and gave me two kisses. He could barely speak when I introduced them to each other. A waiter brought the soup course. "Oh, my God! There's Vivien Leigh." He grabbed a napkin and took out his pen. "I'm too excited to eat. I'm going to mingle." David wandered off, leaving me alone at the table.

I was having trouble with my fake eyelashes. One of them fell into the soup. I took out my hand mirror to stick it back on, but after a few failed attempts I gave up, took off the other one, and threw them both into the ashtray. "A person could go blind wearing these things," I muttered.

I looked up and watched Lee hopping from table to table, my eyes following his every move. Then I noticed a sexy brunette was also tracking his course. At one point, he came over to her and whispered in her ear. She smiled up at him.

David returned to the table with a puzzled look and showed me a strange signature. "I thought the guy was John Wayne," he said. "Boy, this is some shindig."

I sighed. "To tell you the truth, I've never felt comfortable at these things."

After we got home and David left, I ripped off my wardrobe, went into the master bathroom, and took a long look in the mirror. "What a waste," I told myself and scrubbed off my new face. In bed Lee took me in his arms and studied me carefully. "Now, in this light I see the difference. You look beautiful." He pulled me into him and we made love. "God, I love you," he called out at the height of our passion. We lay embraced, energy spent. "Come to London," he whispered in my ear. "It's time we put some romance back into this marriage."

"What about the kids? I promised I'd take them and their friends to the lodge over spring break."

"Take them after you get back." He took my face in his hands. "Don't forget, the kids are here because of us. We come first."

While Lee began to snore, I lay awake staring at the ceiling.

Lee had been gone a month, and I was due to fly to London and spend ten days with him. We spoke frequently on the phone, but imagining our time together made me anxious.

Sorting through the day's mail the day before packing to leave, I picked up *The Hollywood Reporter* and scanned the news until a bit of gossip caught my attention.

"Who is the beautiful Brit keeping Lee Marvin company while he's in London shooting *The Dirty Dozen*?"

Damn it, Lee, I thought. *You just can't keep your fly closed, can you? "Put some romance back in this marriage," he says. What marriage?*

Lee called that evening. "Hi, sweetheart."

"Hello, Lee."

"Can't wait for you to get here."

"I'm not so sure I'm coming."

"What do you mean? I need you here."

"Don't you think it'll be a little crowded?"

"What are you talking about?"

"I just read in the trades you're not lacking for female company. And I don't feel like sharing."

"Oh, honey, how can you believe that rag? You know they'll print anything to sell papers. Please come. I want you here. I miss you."

I hung up, full of doubts. Finally I called him back.

"I'll come, but I want my own place."

"What?"

"I would be more comfortable if you stay at your mews house in Knightsbridge and rent me a hotel room."

"Whatever you say. Just get over here."

I hung up and waited for my breath to come back.

Early in the morning, as the plane landed at Heathrow Airport, I took out my compact. Fresh lipstick, a moment of contemplation, and I was off the plane. *What in the hell am I doing here? Keep an open mind,* I told myself. *Give him another chance.*

I didn't see Lee in the waiting crowd outside the gates. *Probably he didn't want to be spotted,* I thought. I started walking toward baggage claim.

"Hey there, beautiful," someone whispered from behind me, putting a hand on my waist. I wheeled around and it was Lee, obviously drunk. When he put his arms around me for a kiss, I was turned off and pulled back. His breath, even his clothes, reeked of gin.

"Don't be like that, honey," he implored.

"You're drunk."

"No, I . . . Okay, I had one. That's it. I was so excited about your coming . . . And now that you're here, all I want to do is celebrate!"

"Well, let's celebrate over breakfast. I'm starved."

Lee had made reservations for me at the Dorchester, and after checking in we ordered a full breakfast, starting off with a couple of gin fizzes.

"Don't you have to be on the set?" I asked him ruefully. *God*, I thought, *this is familiar*. I had him out the door, avoiding his kiss, and was finally happy to be left alone in the beautiful suite he had reserved.

I didn't see Lee again until three days later, when he took me to dinner followed by an evening of casual sex. After that we saw each other only spasmodically. He was working long hours and spending a great deal of his free time at the local pub. I was pretty much on my own; but a few friends who lived in London kept me from being lonely, and I was entertained by other members of the cast. Gena and John Cassavetes had a built-in family—members of John's production company who heard I was on my own and came to my rescue. They might have felt sorry for me, but we had fun nevertheless.

One evening, Lee and I went to a dinner party at the home of *The Dirty Dozen* director, Robert Aldrich, where I ran into Robert Ryan, an old buddy from Hollywood for SANE days. He, as the others, knew Lee and I were having problems.

"At the sake of sounding crass, Betty dear, I wouldn't dump this marriage too quickly. I see what the deal is, but if you leave Lee, you'll just end up marrying another version of the same man. They're all alike."

"All of you?" I joked, trying to lighten the moment. But back at the hotel I wondered if Robert had a point. I was looking forward to getting home and back to my analysis. I needed to get my head straight.

Just back from London, I was unpacking when the phone rang. It was my friend Bev calling from New York.

"So how was your trip?"

"Don't ask. I didn't see that much of Lee. He was drinking as usual. Frankly, I had more fun without him than with him."

"Did you two talk about your problems?"

"He doesn't think we have any."

"He must be sleepwalking."

"I don't know what's going on," I said, "but it smells like an affair. Of course he denies it. I tried to get him to talk to me, but I couldn't get through to him."

"I'm sorry, Betty, but I'm not really surprised. Hang in there, sweetie. I'm coming out." Bev's marriage had ended the year before due to her husband's drinking and infidelity. Perhaps she could teach me a thing or two.

A week later Bev arrived from New York. That evening we were having a drink by the fire. The kids had been fed and were asleep.

"I'm starved," she said. "What time do you usually have dinner?"

"It depends. If Lee and I are together and he's coming home, I wait and eat with him."

"And how often is that, pray tell? More importantly, why do you do it?"

"I don't know. It's hard to break bad habits."

"No comment. Tell me about your trip."

"I loved London. I must have stopped into every gallery and bookshop in town. And the theater—"

"And . . . ?" Bev interjected.

"Well, I had my chances, Bev, just not with my husband. He was mostly unavailable. Big surprise! But the funny thing is . . . there were men. Nothing serious. I just mean, everywhere I went, men asked me out or seemed to want to be with me."

"Maybe you're just finally noticing!"

"Oh, please." But it was true. I rarely thought of myself with another man all the years of my marriage.

It had been a month since Lee and I had been together in London. By now, I was dreading his return. I decided perhaps a new outfit would lift my spirits. Might as well let him see me at my best, even though I was feeling my worst. If we were going to go our separate ways, I would give him something attractive to remember me by. He wasn't the only actor in the family.

I didn't feel like driving into Beverly Hills to Jax, the only chic boutique in Los Angeles with all of Rudi's collection. In my state of mind I'd better stick to Westwood, and that meant Bullock's. I never cared too much about shopping when times were good, so now I wanted to put as little time and energy into it as possible. I picked out several outfits and found a dressing room. With little enthusiasm, I took off my cotton knit pants and shirt and put on a black linen sheath. After struggling to zip up the back, I looked in the mirror and realized the dress was practically a copy of one already in my closet. *Perhaps I should try this red jersey*, I thought. *The color might pick me up, give me some strength to do what I have to do.*

The sound of two voices sharing excited conversation and laughter in the next dressing room interrupted my thoughts. These women were obviously having fun. Perhaps their exuberance would take away some of my sadness. I listened more carefully.

"Ya think this is sexy enough?" one asked.

"What difference does it make? You're not gonna have it on that long anyway," the other voice answered. They both laughed. It sounded like a good time ahead.

"God, I can't wait to get my hands on that man. It's been too long. I don't know how I've stood it. Maybe I should get both of these. He can afford it. Do you like this color on me?"

"I like you better in black, but it's great for your figure. Your tits look huge."

"They are. That's what he likes, tits and ass." Again, much laughter.

Somewhat shocked by their vulgarity, I looked at the reflection of my small breasts and hips and felt another pang of despair. As I listened intently to what sounded like a couple of hookers getting ready to score, I realized what a sheltered life I had led as a woman. It had been a long time since I had felt attractive, let alone sexy.

Then I overheard the first voice say, "When he called last night he told me I was his one and only. He doesn't want me to come to the airport. He said the limo will bring him right to the beach."

"Does that mean his marriage is over?" the other voice asked.

"I'm afraid to ask. I hope so. I've waited this long. I'll wait as long as I have to. He doesn't want to be married, but he loves his kids. His wife's a real ball breaker."

This woman isn't your run-of-the-mill call girl, I thought. *She's some husband's mistress, waiting for his marriage to end.* A familiar chord struck. This could be the mistress in my marriage—in the very next room! I fell into a chair on top of my clothes.

Was my imagination playing tricks on me? The fantasy took over and panic set in. *She mustn't find me here.* I checked to be sure the dressing room door was locked. *I'm now the mistress, hiding in the background. We have traded places. Why am I buying a new dress? Am I still competing for my husband's love when I don't want him anymore? But I do want him. I want him to be the man I married, the man who loves me and only me.*

When Lee returned we never talked about what happened in London. He went on acting as if I were the only woman in his life, but I knew we were in trouble.

After he'd been back home for a week, Lee was called back to the set of *Ship of Fools* for additional dubbing.

Our friend Larry Hagman phoned out of the blue to see how things were going. He knew Lee was playing around and, being a happily married man, took a dim view of his antics. He invited the kids and me to go out to lunch. While waiting for our orders, the children got into their usual sibling rivalry while Larry continued his best friend therapy. "I don't know what it is about this business, but marriages just don't survive."

"What about Jimmy and Gloria Stewart?" I said.

"What about Betty and Keenan Wynn?" he countered.

"What about them?

"That was some marriage," he said. "Betty ran off with Donald O'Connor. Then Gwen divorced Donald and married Dan Dailey. In the meantime, Keenan married Evie, who then ran off with his best friend, Van Johnson."

"No!

"Yes! Where have you been?"

"Oh, look, there's Daddy!" Claudia called out excitedly.

We all looked over to the corner booth and saw Lee huddled with the sexy brunette I remembered from Chasen's. When he spotted us, he got up and made a dash for the emergency exit. The door was locked. He looked like a trapped animal. Reluctantly, he came over to our table before the kids could get to his.

"What a surprise!" he said, faking composure.

"Who's the lady, Daddy?" Claudia said, pointing to his companion, who was slinking down in the other booth.

"She works with Daddy on the movie."

"What does she do with you?"

Larry gave Lee an icy look. "Yeah, what does she do with you?"

Lee ignored him and looked at his watch. "Jesus, we're late. Gotta get back to the set. I'll call you later, sweetheart." He leaned down, gave me a kiss, and was out the door, the mystery woman trailing behind.

Larry could see I was shaken.

"Everybody go get ice cream," he said to the kids, handing Christopher a twenty. The kids ran off to the counter.

"Who is she?" I said.

"Sorry, Betty. Everyone knows her. She's a real pro. Beats me how he can play around with a dame who has fucked most of Hollywood when he's got you and the kids." I hushed him as the kids returned to the table.

"Can we go see Daddy play with the lady?" Claudia said.

"No, darling, time for your nap. We're going home," I said.

21

Waking Up from a Bad Dream

A few weeks later I heard the phone ringing as I came in the side door. I had just returned from my carpool chore, the late afternoon pickup of Christopher from Boy Scouts, Courtenay from her violin lesson, and Cynthia from dance. Chauffeuring children, four of my own and numerous neighbors, seemed an endless task. I raced upstairs to the master bedroom, threw off my coat, kicked off my shoes, and grabbed the phone on my bedside table.

"Hello," I said, somewhat out of breath.

"Betty?"

I paused, trying to distinguish the caller. "Speaking."

"This is Mishell." This was a strange woman's voice.

"Mishell? I'm afraid I don't know you."

"Oh, come on, Betty, you know who I am. I'm Lee's mistress."

I said nothing.

"Betty, are you there?" she asked after several beats.

"There must be some mistake. Why are you calling me? What do you want?" I asked, not recognizing my own voice. Hands trembling, heart pounding, I dropped the receiver. My knees collapsed and I sank to the bed. Recovering the phone, I mumbled, "Sorry." What was I apologizing for? Being out of control? I attempted to regain composure. "But I really don't know who you are."

"Betty, don't you think it's time we talk? I'm going to marry Lee. Your marriage is over."

Feeling faint, I excused myself and hung up. I don't know how long I lay on the bed trying to collect my thoughts. It was dark when the children came up to ask about dinner. I heard them, but I couldn't answer.

"What's wrong, Mom?" Christopher asked, tenuously. He sounded so small.

"I'm sorry, honey," I said. "I'll be right down." I pulled myself together, went to the kitchen, and, in a trance, threw together some dinner. The children ate quietly, knowing something was wrong. Afterward, I retreated to my room.

I lay back down on my bed in the dark and felt nothing. That frightened me. I dreaded the delayed reaction that was bound to come.

I called Lee's agent. "Meyer, I'm sorry to bother you, but who is Mishell?"

"Oh, God, what happened?" he asked.

"She called here and introduced herself. What's going on?"

"Betty, I'm sorry that tramp called you. I'll call Lee at the studio and he'll be home soon. Please don't do anything. Don't worry. Everything will be fine."

Almost as soon as I'd hung up, the phone rang again. It was Meyer. "Betty, I talked with Lee and he'll be home in an hour. He loves you and is very upset that Mishell called. Everything will be all right. You'll see."

Less than an hour later, I heard Lee's car pull into the garage. I shuddered. *What kind of story is he going to hand me now?* I wondered as I came down the stairs. But Lee was silent, eyes downcast. When he finally lifted his head, he murmured, "Please forgive me." Our eyes locked. All our years together passed between us in one look. We knew the damage had been done.

"I forgive you," I said. "But I don't want you here. You have to go."

The beginning of the end

The next evening I explained to the kids that their father and I had decided to live apart for a while. They seemed sad over the news but did not want to talk about it.

Life was calmer with Lee out of the house, staying in a motel, the waves stirred only when he'd suddenly stop by. As time went on, the memory of the night we parted seemed to slip from him, and he became more flirtatious – teasing and touching

When my father called to tell us he had bought an avocado ranch and moved to San Diego, I told him Lee and I had separated. Daddy jumped into his car and in a few hours was at my door.

"What time is Lee coming home?" he asked. "I want to talk to him."

"I told you, Daddy. Lee's not living here anymore. We're separated."

"You better think this over, kiddo. Lee's given you a wonderful life, everything money could buy. What more could you want?" I turned away and stifled a scream. "I need a drink," he said and went to the bar.

I followed him. "Daddy, try to get this through your head. If you want to talk to Lee, I'll give you his number. He is not welcome here anymore."

At that moment Lee burst through the door. "Hi, Chief. How're you doin'?" He came over to give me a kiss. "Hi, sweetheart."

I pulled away. "Don't 'sweetheart' me. What are you doing here?"

Lee looked to Daddy. "She's mad at me," he said with a wink. Then he turned back to me. "We're gonna work it out, aren't we, baby?"

I ignored him and turned to my father. "Will you tell him to get out of here and go back to his mistress?"

"There's no pleasing some women," said Lee, reaching for me. "C'mere, baby."

I hauled off and hit him. Being always so well behaved, I shocked myself. But it was a moment I had been waiting for and it felt great.

"Jesus!" Lee yelled.

"She can be very temperamental," my father said as Lee backed out the door.

The house was too big, too empty, and too quiet for a Sunday. The children had gone to the beach house Lee had bought to spend the day with their father. I missed them and their friends—their squeals and laughter while jumping into the pool, dripping down the back hallway, running showers, snapping towels, and slamming doors. I walked down the hall and peeked into their bedrooms, noticing a stray sock left on the floor, pajamas on the foot of a bed, a game of tic-tac-toe on a closet door blackboard. It was eleven in the morning, and they had been gone a long two hours.

It would be another six hours until their return. How would I get through the day? My missing them was laced with concern. How would they manage in their father's care at his beach house? He had never spent one day alone with them. I knew in my heart he was still seeing Mishell. Would she be there? He wouldn't dare expose them to that trashy dame, would he? What would he do with them all day? I hoped he wouldn't start drinking. What if a pal dropped by for a beer?

Trying not to worry, I spent the next hour filling the house with fresh roses from the garden and watering the indoor plants. I looked around at this perfect home for the ideal family. It was all a sham. What a fool I had been for believing my marriage vows.

I climbed the stairs and went into Lee's dressing room, something I had done every day for ten years, gathering or putting away his laundry. I looked through the French windows down into the beautiful garden with the old oak trees. *Strong as an oak, that's what I must be*, I told myself. I turned, opened one of the doors, and pulled out a rack of his beautifully tailored jackets in shades of gray and tan. I fondled the charcoal cashmere and put my cheek to the soft fabric faintly scented with 4711. My tears fell on the sleeve. I embraced the jacket for some time, still feeling my lover's body inside. Then, like an unwelcome intruder, I withdrew.

Get out of this house, I told myself. I made several attempts to cover my red, swollen eyes with makeup, finally hiding them behind dark glasses. The phone rang on my way out the door. *Let the service get it*, I thought, then remembered the children.

"Hi, sweetheart." Lee's familiar voice cut through my heart.

"Is everything all right?" I asked.

"Fine. The kids and I thought you might like to come up for lunch." The invitation was tempting.

"I don't think that's a good idea," I answered.

There was a pause. "Well, what shall I feed them?"

Son of a bitch, I thought, *he's looking for a cook*. "Oh, God, give them peanut butter sandwiches. Take them out for hamburgers. Figure it out!" I slammed down the phone.

Driving down San Vincente with the top down, I felt the sun on my back, but my hands were cold as ice. *I'll stop at Brentwood Pharmacy and buy myself a present. It'll cheer me up.* Standing in the perfume section, trying to find a scent that would lift my spirits, I saw Sharley Wynn approaching. I wasn't in the mood to talk to anyone, but she moved in and gave me a hug.

"Oh, darling, I'm so sad about you and Lee."

I had nothing to say. I knew Keenan had long been unfaithful to her, but she didn't seem to care. If only I could be that way, but I knew I couldn't. I mumbled thanks and got out of there.

When I arrived home Lee and the kids were waiting for me.

"Hi, sweetheart, the kids and I want you to come with us to see the sunset."

Cornered, I got into the car and we took off. Lee put his hand on my thigh as we drove through the Marina. He drove on to our favorite family restaurant. I wasn't in the mood for this charade but went along with it for the sake of our children.

The moment we returned home the kids shouted, "Lassie!" and jumped out of the car, running into the playroom to see their favorite TV program. Once we were alone, Lee took my hand. "I still love you. Please don't shut me out. I need you and the kids." His eyes filled with tears. "Please, I beg you, let me come home."

"Okay," I sighed. In spite of the fact I was inviting disaster, I was not yet ready to untie the knot. I still thought of myself as Mrs. Lee Marvin. I needed to be married. I needed to play the successful movie star's wife. Without that I didn't know who I was.

Lee moved back in and his career continued to rise. He won the British Academy Award for *The Killers.* Shortly thereafter *Ship of Fools* opened, earning him the National Board of Review of Motion Pictures Best Actor Award. It also brought together the cast, with memories of our summer at the beach. I had a wonderful but brief reunion with Simone.

Lee was soon sent the script for *Cat Ballou.* Script reading, boring at best, was not Lee's thing, so it was usually left to me. He came into the playroom that afternoon and found me laughing out loud as I turned the pages. I grabbed him on his way to the bar. "Okay!" he said, as I pulled him down to sit by me, talking a mile a minute. "Slow down. Mmm, you smell good." He leaned in for a kiss.

"Stop. Stop, just for a minute, Lee. You've got to do this picture."

"Sweetheart, it's only a little independent flick. There's no money up front. I'd have to defer my salary. Is this blouse new?" He made for the top button. I pulled back, just a little.

"Lee, listen. This script is really funny. How often do you get a chance to do a good comedy? And not one character, but two?

"Okay, okay. Slow down. Let me make a drink and we'll read it together." For the next couple of hours we sat curled up with the script, kicking around ideas for his characters, until Lee agreed it was a perfect showcase for him.

As much as I was involved with his decision to star in the film, he was lost to me once the shooting began. I heard little from him while he was on location, except for a few drunken phone calls. *Cat Ballou* was tailor-made for him, the lead character being an outrageous, lovable drunk. He was barely sober throughout the two-week shoot.

When he returned from location, things seemed fine, for a little while. Lee continued to drink but was loving to me and doted on the children—when he saw them. I had started to make peace with taking him back into our home when one afternoon he called me up into the master bedroom, bathed in sunlight streaming through the bay window.

"This is nothing personal, Betty." He stared out at the garden. "But I don't want to be married anymore."

I was stunned. We sat in silence for some time before I spoke. "I wish I had known about this four kids ago."

"These things happen, sweetheart. It's nobody's fault. You're a terrific wife and a wonderful mother. I just don't want to be married."

Lee kills the marriage

Something in me finally snapped. Full of rage, I jumped up and started throwing everything I could get my hands on.

"Wait a minute. Calm down, will ya?" he pleaded as he ducked and dodged.

"Get out!" I yelled. "Take your stuff and get out of my house."

"Wait a minute! This is my house too!" he yelled, retreating.

"Not anymore. Out! Get out, you son of a bitch!"

He left the room and moved back into his place at the beach.

22

The Final Big Blow

Strangely, I had a sense of relief that something that had been over a long time ago was finally ending. But telling the kids again was hard.

"Are we going to stay in the house?" Christopher asked. "Will we see Dad?"

"Of course you will. Things won't change that much."

"Dad's never here anyway," Courtenay said.

"Shut up, Courtenay! Dad's not here because he's working to support us!" Christopher shouted.

"Christopher, don't say 'shut up' to your sister," I interrupted. "Now, let's all calm down. It's not a happy time, but we're going to be fine. We all have to help each other."

"Mommy, may I have more dessert?" Claudia said, seemingly oblivious.

"I'll get it," said Cynthia, her constant helper.

I could hardly wait to get to bed.

I was determined to get rid of the mink coat plus the diamond and a few other expensive gifts Lee had given me over the years. The multi-diamond ring was a cinch. When the cleaning crew came, it disappeared with the dust, and I collected the insurance. Unloading the coat was not so easy. I took it everywhere, usually dragging it behind me, just to leave it, lose it, or have it stolen. No luck. Restaurants, hotels, airports, cabs always sent it back. Finally I put it at the back of my closet, out of sight and out of mind.

Lee continued to drop by whenever he felt like it, to use the phone or john or to raid the refrigerator. I was fed up with these impromptu visits but wasn't sure what to do about it. Whenever I confronted him, he'd either laugh it off or blow up in anger, which frightened the kids. The rules I had laid down to protect my privacy were ignored.

Christmas was around the corner, but the kids argued against going away, hoping instead to spend the holidays with their friends. I was torn, wanting to keep them happy, yet needing a break from Latimer Road. I was at the tennis courts, my usual haunt, and ran into Hal Holbrook. He mentioned he was looking for a house to rent while relocating from New York.

"Why don't you take my place?" I said.

"I didn't know it was available."

"Oh, I've been thinking about the kids and I spending a few months at the beach." I didn't want to get into the details of Lee and myself. I took Hal back to the house and showed him around. We agreed he could move in the following week.

Our move fell into place quickly. Dan O'Herlihy offered me his home in Malibu Colony for six months while he went east to do a play. When I went to check it out, I felt a sense of security as I gave my name to the patrol outside the gated community, with its private street and tennis courts. I walked around his three-story sunlit house, hearing the waves hit the shore outside, and imagined the kids and me living there, our first home without Lee. The comfortable, casual living room with overstuffed sofas and glassed-in porch to the beach was inviting. The master suite and three bedrooms on the second floor offered me privacy, yet kept me close to the girls. I would give Christopher the third floor so he could have his newly formed rock band practice without driving the rest of us crazy. It seemed like a good move, even though it was temporary.

When the kids came home from school, I broke the news.

"This way you can have a holiday on the beach with your pals. You have friends living in the Colony."

"What about when school starts?" they asked.

"I'll arrange a car pool with other students going to Oakwood. Christopher, you can go to Malibu High for a semester if you want."

Nobody really argued very much. Within a week, Hal was living in our house, and the kids and I had packed a few things and moved to Malibu. A lightness of being settled over us for those first quiet days.

The following week, the Oscar nominations for 1965 were announced. It had been a huge year for Lee: *Ship of Fools* was nominated for Best

Film, among many other nominations for the picture, and to everyone's surprise, Lee received his first Academy Award nomination for Best Actor, for his work in *Cat Ballou*.

Hal called me from the Latimer Road house. It seems Lee had walked in, unannounced as always, and found Hal in the playroom. Hal explained that I'd rented him the place to him and had moved to the beach. Hal said Lee had seemed surprised, and he hoped it was all right that he'd given him my address. I said it was fine, knowing it was just a matter of time before Lee caught up with me.

Lee sauntered into my Malibu hideaway, too excited about his nomination to even mention my abrupt change of residence.

"Two films in one year. You know I hate awards, but this is going to be some evening, sweetheart. I want you to have the most beautiful gown you can find. Maybe have Galanos design something special for you. You look terrific in his things. It's going to be a great night."

I couldn't believe my ears. How could he be carrying on about a gown when our marriage was ending? "I'll think about it, Lee." My response took the wind out of his sails and he left quietly. The kids were at school, and I didn't tell them their father had been there. The phone rang shortly afterward.

"Betty, hi." After so many years, I knew Meyer Mishkin's voice immediately. "Hello, Meyer. Did Lee give you this number?"

"Just talked to him. As a matter of fact, that's the reason for my call. I know you two are, well, sorting things out, but the press is terrible. I'm sure you've seen the papers."

"Actually, I've been trying to avoid them."

"Don't blame you. But it might calm things down if you and Lee show up together at the Awards. I don't mean to interfere, Betty, but one good photo of Mr. and Mrs. Lee Marvin would shut some people up."

I hated the kids being exposed to all the claptrap printed about their parents' separation and took Meyer's words to heart. I ordered a hand-beaded, form-fitting, full-length gown to wear to the ceremony. There was a second reason for my accepting Lee's invitation to attend. I had been there every step of the way in his career, and I wanted to be with him on the biggest night of his professional life.

Our plans were set. A few days before the Awards, Lee showed up at the beach, unannounced. "I have to talk to you," he said, pacing up and down.

"What is it?"

"Sweetheart, you're not going to believe this. I don't know what to do."

"What's wrong?"

"Mishell's threatening to kill herself if I don't take her to the Awards."

"Sounds good to me."

"You don't understand. I'm serious. She means it. You've gotta help me out here. That woman's crazy."

"What do you want me to do, Lee?"

"Would you be okay watching at home with the kids?" His words came out in a rush.

I didn't know whether to laugh or cry. Every time I thought Lee had sunk as low as he could go, he went even lower.

"Will you be all right at home?" he asked again.

"Do you really care?"

I tried to make light of the turn in events to the kids, but there really wasn't any hiding from them what Lee had done. The evening of the Awards, we all sat on my bed together watching the broadcast. Lee and Mishell made their entrance—she flaunting her Valentino gown, he in a black leather tuxedo. I couldn't believe my eyes. He'd gone totally Hollywood.

Lee was being pulled from all sides. At least he corrected a naïve reporter who referred to Mishell as "Mrs. Marvin."

"Ya got that wrong, buddy. Mrs. Marvin is under the weather and couldn't make it. She's at home with my four beautiful children."

And so I was.

The crowd at the Awards applauded and the kids cheered when their father won. Lee stood and reached across Mishell to shake Meyer's hand, then went on stage to thank a horse somewhere in the valley, ignoring the many people who were responsible for his success. I sat quietly and watched. I was touched by Dr. Rangell's phone call of concern during the ceremony.

Immediately after the Awards the phone rang again. It was Lee. "Sweetheart, I just called to tell you I love you. You're the first one I thought of when I won. I owe this all to you."

I hung up. The next day my beach neighbor and new friend, Robert Brown, sent a large bunch of beautiful flowers with a handwritten note: "Here's to the lovely woman behind the man."

No more, I thought.

23

Breaking Out of Prison

When the kids and I moved back to Latimer Road, I started looking for an attorney and told Lee I was getting a divorce.

"You'll regret this. Don't do it," he warned. "Maybe you should have an affair. I think that's what you need. I can't believe you never had anyone else the whole time we've been married. It might have helped."

"Me or you? You think two wrongs make a right? No, Lee, I'm glad I was faithful to you. One less thing to feel bad about. But I can't live this way anymore. Besides, I believe you were telling the truth when you said you didn't want to be married."

"I'm telling you, Betty, don't get a divorce. You may not know it now, but after me, there's no one. You and I will always be together. We're man and wife."

"The perfect dream. What about your mistress?"

"Oh, she won't be any trouble. I'll keep her at the beach. As a matter of fact, you two should get to know each other. You might even become friends."

"That's the sickest thing I've ever heard!"

"In Europe men have always had mistresses. Their wives don't seem to mind."

"Well, I'm American and I do. Call your attorney."

I painted every day. It was my only escape and I needed one badly. But there was really no getting away from what was raging inside me. The images on the canvas were aggressive, dark, and foreboding. Their appearance made me sick to my stomach, literally.

The next day, while driving the white Ford station wagon, I realized I had grown to hate everything that car represented. It was the all-American housewife/young mother's vehicle for hauling kids and groceries. It was time to change my image. I saw a sexy blonde zipping around the turns on Sunset in an eggplant-colored Buick Riviera. *Now, that beauty is about as far away from the "domesticated female on wheels" look as one could get,* I thought. I went right down to the Buick dealer, dropped off the Ford, and drove out in a Riviera, identical to the one I had seen. When I got home I called our business manager, Ed Silver, and told him the news.

"How much did it cost?" he asked, our money being his main concern.

"Would you believe I only had to give them the Ford and $23?"

"No, I wouldn't," he said. "I'll call them and take care of it."

I'd signed papers to finance the car without a clue as to what I was doing. It was the first time in years I had made a move on my own financially, and I definitely had a lot to learn.

My attempts to change my image did not stop with the car. One day I caught a glimpse of myself getting out of the shower. I studied my small breasts and decided implants would make me look and feel sexier. After one operation I went from a 36A to a 36C. The next time Lee dropped by he couldn't take his eyes off my cleavage.

"Are those your breasts?" he said.

"Absolutely. Bought and paid for."

He shook his head and smiled.

It was time for my mother to make her annual visit, a gift I had given her from 1957, the time Lee and I could afford it. I knew this visit was going to be particularly difficult because she, unaware of our problems, thought Lee was the perfect son-in-law.

On my way to the airport I was so full of anxiety that I was pulled over and ticketed by a traffic cop for going too slow on the freeway.

"Will Lee be coming home for dinner?" my mom asked on our way back.

"I told you on the phone, Mother. Lee is living at the beach. I'm divorcing him." She sat quietly for a while, looking straight ahead. I hoped that would be the end of it. No such luck.

"Betty, don't rush into anything."

Her words made me dizzy, and I had such trouble breathing I feared I might crash.

"I don't think we should discuss this now," I whispered. I made it home and pulled into the garage as the kids were coming in from school. They were the perfect distraction while I regained composure.

Mother and I walked into the courtyard. I was trying to think of how to steer the conversation away from Lee when we turned toward the playroom and saw someone inside fixing himself a drink. It was Daddy. My mother looked first bewildered, then shocked. She hadn't seen him since before I was born.

"Betty! What is he doing here? How could you?"

I couldn't believe this was happening.

"Mother, I swear, I didn't invite him. I'm as surprised as you are. Daddy—my father—comes around sometimes. He doesn't call first. I'm so sorry." I looked at my mother, trying to imagine what she might be feeling. "Do you want to say hello?" I asked gently.

"I have nothing to say to that man," she said and escaped to the guestroom.

I went inside to my father. "Daddy."

"Hey, kiddo!" He reached to embrace me.

"No time for that now, and put down that drink. You have to leave. My mother is here. She doesn't want to see you."

"Why can't she let bygones be bygones? Besides, I'm not here to see her. I want to talk about Lee," Daddy said plaintively. "Where is he?"

"He's not coming by any time soon." I took the glass out of my father's hand and guided him to the door. "I will talk to you about this another time. But not while Mother's visiting. Good-bye, Daddy."

Almost as soon as Daddy had driven off, my mother reappeared.

"What time did you say Lee would be home? Will he be here in time for dinner?"

"Mother, I told you. He's not coming here. He doesn't live here anymore." It was all too much. Both my parents seemed more interested in Lee than in me. I burst into tears. "I'm sorry," I said, grabbing a tissue off the coffee table.

"Oh, Betty," she pleaded, "Please don't cry. I've never seen you cry."

The divorce was a long, humiliating process. I wandered around in a daze most of the time. When Lee realized I was serious about divorcing him and that we would never be together again, his tone changed from assertive to sad. He no longer made idle threats, but seemed resigned to the situation.

"If you insist on going through with this, I promise you and the kids will never want for anything."

Word got out, and attorneys famous for getting big settlements for Hollywood wives phoned to see if they could represent me. I always refused, certain that Lee would keep his word. I liked the attorney I chose and believed that was important. He was sweet, bright, and experienced, but it was quickly evident that he was no match for Lee's legal team. They were determined to protect his future earnings, in spite of Lee wanting to do right by the children and me. After all, they were protecting their own interests.

I knew I was in trouble when the judge called us all into chambers to discuss our differences. He completely ignored me as we entered with our respective legal counsels. His eyes were only on Lee. "Hello, Mr. Marvin!" he said. "Before we get started, I just want to tell you how much I've enjoyed all your movies. I'm a big fan."

Oh, brother. Not a good sign, I thought.

My attorney did his best to argue on my behalf, but the die was already cast. Not only was I being faced with the possibility of serious financial trouble, but any privacy the kids and I had had was shot to hell. The press was having a field day. Reporters had no hesitation about calling the house at any hour of the day or night, audacious in asking personal questions. I always answered, "No comment." On days that some trade paper or magazine had a particularly cruel piece of gossip about Lee and his live-in mistressI kept the kids home from school. They were suffering enough without being teased.

When Lee left home, Christopher was fourteen, an adolescent left behind in an all-female household, with a mother, three younger sisters, and our housekeeper, Anna. Concerned about the lack of an adult male presence at home, I considered sending Christopher to a boarding school. He and I were driving back to our house after an appointment with a school counselor to discuss our options.

"Mom, am I bad?" he said.

"Why no, honey, quite the opposite. You're the best boy I know."

"Then why are you sending me away?" He was fighting to hold back the tears.

"Oh, Christopher, I just want to take some of the pressure off you. I thought you would like to get away from your sisters and me."

"Please don't send me away."

I stopped the car. "That's it. You're not going anywhere."

"Thanks, Mom." We dried our eyes. I put some music on the radio as we drove home, a newfound peace settling between my son and me. Instead of sending Christopher away to school, I hired Mr. Brody, a caring teacher, to come to the house and tutor him several times a week. He became the perfect temporary surrogate father to my son.

While my world was falling apart, the attorneys were matter-of-factly counting the assets and negotiating how to best cut up the pie. I foolishly had thought Lee's legal team were my friends all the years they had represented us. Now they hardly acknowledged me. I learned quickly that our divorce would be all about money. Lee's promise that I would want for nothing was pushed aside as they fought to keep as much of his present and future earnings as possible. I made no demands, and my nice attorney was no shark. As a result, the children's needs were not protected, and I had no claim to any of Lee's future earnings. I received the house and lifetime alimony, but little child support, as it was not tax-deductible. I did not fight the settlement. I had no fight left.

Without emotion, I resolutely signed the final divorce papers in 1965 and called it a day. My attorney drove me home, and I sat alone in the playroom waiting for a wave of despair to settle over me, but it didn't come.

An hour or more later, I was still sitting there when Lee walked in, came over, and put his arms around me. An air of guilt hung over him, knowing he had allowed his attorneys to protect his future from his past. I felt nothing.

"Sweetheart, this was a horrible day for both of us."

I did not respond as he continued. "Those attorneys have to do their job, but no matter what the divorce papers say, I'll always take care of you and the kids."

My silence sent him on his way.

24

Packing Up and Moving On

It had started out to be fun—an Easter vacation in 1967 with the kids spent skiing with friends at Mammoth Mountain. The snow was getting soft, but we skied through the week, junk and all. On Good Friday, the last run of the season, I was foolishly still in my racing bindings, coming down a gentle slope on the back of run three.

"Mom, watch me parallel ski," called Cynthia from up above. I turned around, slipped back into some junk, lost my balance, and sat down unexpectedly, watching my left leg twist around in slow motion. There was not enough impact for the ski to come off, and I knew when I saw blood the leg had been fractured.

An ambulance took me to the local hospital for surgery. I was pretty much out of it the following day until I found myself being transported by hospital plane to Santa Monica. Lee had been contacted and had decided it was better for me to be home, near the children. I wasn't consulted, but then I was in no shape to discuss much. Lee was waiting with an ambulance to take me back to the house. After tucking me into bed, he went back to the beach, leaving me with the children, a broken leg, and no assistance.

As soon as the medication wore off, I was in agony. By the middle of the night I could stand it no longer and called my doctor. Within an hour the same two young men who had brought me home a few hours before arrived and reversed the plan, carrying me back down the stairs and delivering me to St. John's Hospital.

I spent the next two months there, undergoing two more operations. A few days after the last surgery, the pain caused from the leg swelling inside the cast became excruciating. Demerol had become dangerously habit

153

forming, and I'd sworn off any pain medication, but this was unbearable. From my hospital bed, I begged the nurse to call the surgeon or at least the doctor on call, but there was no response. When my friend Carol showed up to visit, I told her, "I'm in terrible pain. I need you to do me a favor."

"What is it?"

"Do you have your station wagon with you?" She nodded. "Pull it up outside the emergency exit. Then find a wheelchair in the hall, get me into your car, and drive me over to the doctor's office. Please."

No one asked where I was going as I left the hospital in a wheelchair. With Carol's help I made it to the doctor's office and hobbled into a crowded room on my crutches.

"Since the doctor is too busy to see me, I've come to see him," I called to the receptionist. Sensing my determination, she immediately showed me into a private room. "Get this damn thing off my leg!" I shouted at the doctor when he put his head in the door. Without a word he got his saw, removed the cast, and put on a looser one, and I returned to the hospital. I hadn't even been missed.

Two weeks later I was released and went home with a full leg cast, confined to a hospital bed that had been set up in the playroom. The kids were relieved to have me home, and I was looking forward to getting the cast off and starting physical therapy. But in the meantime I needed help, and that evening friends came over to barbecue for the kids and me. After dinner, when the guests had left and the kids were in bed, I was aware of discomfort in my chest. I took something for indigestion and fell asleep.

In the middle of the night I awakened, unable to breathe. I couldn't figure out what was happening to me and didn't want to disturb the doctor at that hour, so I sat on the edge of the bed gasping until dawn. When I finally did phone him, apologizing for the disturbance, he called an ambulance immediately and they rushed me, once again, back to St. John's Hospital, this time into intensive care. I had a pulmonary embolism from a clot that had broken free from my last surgery and had traveled to my lungs.

For the next ten days I hung in a delicate balance between life and death. Lee and our children stayed by my bed. When I was able to focus enough to really look into their eyes, I could see the fear in their faces.

"Claudia, come here," I said. My nine-year-old daughter stood at the far end of the bed and would not come near me. "Don't be afraid, darling. Mommy's going to be fine." Claudia stood frozen to the spot, and I could see she was crying. I struggled to maintain lucidity, but I knew at that moment I was beginning to slip away. *You can't leave your children now,* I kept telling myself, *They need you.* Sheer determination saved my life.

Finally the clot was dissolved, and I was transferred from intensive care to a private room in the hospital, where I spent another ten days getting my strength back, my leg still in a full-length cast. The cast was still on when I was sent home to begin the long recovery from the fracture.

After the last leg cast was removed, I spent the next six months in physical therapy. The accident had severed the nerves from the knee down, and I had been told I probably would never have full use of my left leg. *Not on your life,* I told myself. I swam every day in the pool to prove the therapists wrong.

The freedom I felt in the water allowed me to go over what had happened to me. My marriage to Lee was truly over. I could feel myself moving past it as I swam back and forth, lap after lap. The accident had forced me to slow down and take inventory of my life. I needed to make real changes, and while slowly moving through the water, I began to look beyond the accident and create a survival plan.

First, I was determined to put some real distance between Lee and myself. "I'm moving to Rome," I told him when I saw him next.

"You're what?" He looked at me in astonishment. "You're joking."

"No, I'm quite serious."

"What about the kids?"

"Of course the kids are coming with me."

"When?"

"When school lets out. I've enrolled the girls in schools there, and Christopher's coming back here to college in the fall. I've signed on as part of a team to restore the paintings that were damaged in the Venice flood."

"You've really thought this through, haven't you?"

"I want to get away from this town," I said. "The change will be good for all of us. I've been worried about Christopher, surrounded by wealthy students smoking pot. The inside of the van you gave him to carry his drums around looks like a harem. I'm relieved he's going to college in the fall, now that he's beat the draft."

"I can't understand why you fought to keep him out of the war," Lee said.

"Because the war in Vietnam is a crock. Let's not get into that again. We have better things to fight about."

"Let's talk about us," he said. "Mishell and I are finished. I have moved out."

"But that's your house."

"I know, but the dame won't leave. I told her I wouldn't marry her. So now she has had her name legally changed to Marvin."

"Maybe I should change mine back to Ebeling," I said, laughing. *How desperate can she get*, I thought.

"It's not funny, Betty. My attorneys have to get a court order to have her evicted." "I think you should know she has started using credit cards with 'Mrs. Lee Marvin' on them. I found out when I was shopping at Saks. The stores won't give me credit if I change my name. So now there are two Mrs. Lee Marvin accounts. It's a mess. Also, she has found where I shop and have my hair done. She calls and makes appointments in my name. It's driving everyone crazy, including me."

"I'm so sorry, sweetheart."

"Why did you choose such a dame?" I asked.

"Because I didn't have to talk to her. She was just there."

"I'm sorry for you." I meant it.

"I made a terrible mistake. I wish we could get back together." I shook my head slowly.

"Will you at least think about it?"

"Lee, we're divorced. Someone once said that going back to an ex-husband is like breaking into prison."

I kept my word. In July, 1969, the children and I packed up and sailed on the Raffaello from New York to Genoa.

25

The King and I on a Roman Holiday

"Betty, meet Il Marchese Luigi Bruno di Belmonte III." Nancy and Carroll O'Connor had taken me to a fashionable restaurant to celebrate my arrival in Rome. Il Marchese, the king of Modica, Sicily, bent toward me, took my hand, and kissed it, never taking his beautiful blue eyes away from mine. I had never met a king before and was thrilled. He was short, handsome, and elegantly dressed, with a silk scarf tucked into a pale blue shirt under a tan linen jacket. "Signora Marvin. Welcome to Rome. I heard you were moving here."

"Really," I responded. "And how is that?"

"Word travels fast in certain circles of this village."

Oh, God, I wondered, *has the scandal of my divorce traveled this far?* I came back to his smile and was relieved when he said no more about it.

I couldn't take my eyes off Gigi, as his friends called him. We drew closer and closer together. Eventually the others went home and Gigi swept me from club to club, introducing me to the best Rome had to offer. He drove me back to my flat in the Borghese Gardens, kissed me on both cheeks, announced he was leaving the next day for New York, delivered a parting "Ciao," and was gone.

The next day when I arrived home from delivering the girls to school, our housekeeper, Antoinetta, seemed desperate to give me a message. *"Signora, Il Marchese Luigi Bruno di Belmonte ha telefonato. Signora, Il Marchese, capito?"* The king had called and she could barely contain herself. *"Signora, per favore, Il Marchese."* I was a little thrown by her excitement, but obviously this was a man of importance. I felt a quick rush. Soon the phone rang.

"Betty, this is Gigi." So now we were on a first name basis. Good.

"I thought you were on your way to New York."

"I decided that could wait until after we have dinner."

As soon as I hung up the phone rang again. I picked it up.

"Pronto?"

"Pronto yourself, sweetheart." That familiar, seductive voice gave me a rush. I sat down.

"Oh, hi, Lee."

"How's life in Rome? How're the kids? Do you miss me?"

"We're fine, thank you."

"Well, I miss you, and I'm coming over in a couple of weeks."

Panic set in. "I'll see you then," I said and hung up.

I called regularly about going to the conservatory to begin work on the restoration program, but the masterpieces had not yet arrived from Venice. I was disappointed, hoping to throw myself into hard work doing what I had grown to love—painting. I was beginning to realize a lot of Italian projects took place *domani*, tomorrow.

Gigi and I began seeing each other every day. Before I knew it I was caught up in a whirlwind of socializing with aristocrats. Gigi dressed me in a collection from his favorite designers and hired a tutor to improve my Italian. "Those snobs at the club are never going to accept you unless you speak perfectly."

Gigi and I in Rome, 1969

As Lee's visit became imminent, my apprehension grew. I was torn between my own fear that being with him would draw me back into what was, and knowing the girls should see their father.

One evening I was brushing my teeth while listening to the international news in the background. When I heard the name "Lee Marvin," I rushed to the TV and saw his face on the screen. The report was in Italian, but I could piece it together: a whirlwind second marriage. Lee had run into an old girlfriend from years ago and suddenly tied the knot. I sat down on the bed in disbelief, still holding my toothbrush, as the newscast went on to other stories.

Over the next few days I learned, through family and friends, what had happened. Lee had postponed his trip to Italy when he heard his father was dying and had gone up to Woodstock to be with him. Perhaps running into Pam, a woman he'd dated when he was just out of the service and still living upstate, brought him some comfort. At any rate, the report was true. Without a word to anyone, Lee had remarried.

When the shock wore off, I went into mourning. I realized that despite his behavior, including this last topper, I still loved him.

I was happy when Aunt Rella came for an extended visit. It was so good to have someone from home, and Cynthia and Claudia adored her. Having Rella there also allowed me to feel less guilty about leaving them to be with Gigi.

I remained intrigued by him, but soon realized I was merely another possession in his collection of wives and mistresses. He had two of each. As time went on he became more demanding. Being a good Italian boy, he lived with his mother in Rome but kept flats in Paris and London, in addition to his palace and villa in Modica. He expected me to go to any one of them with him whenever he chose.

One weekend Gigi and I flew to Palermo and were met at the airport by a chauffeured limousine for the drive to his villa. Our relationship had become strained and we began to argue. "I can't simply drop everything and run off with you every time you have a whim to jump down to Sicily for the weekend or drop into London for dinner."

"Why not?" He seemed confused.

"Because I have responsibilities as a mother and I made a commitment to work in Rome."

"The babies are fine with Aunt Rella and Antoinetta. And forget about that nonsense with the museum. Your only commitment is to Il Marchese." Ignoring me, he leaned forward and spoke in Sicilian to his driver. I was so exasperated that I barely noticed when the limo parked and we were let out onto the street. I was brought back to reality when the villagers bowed and even dropped to their knees as we approached. Barely acknowledging them, Gigi turned to me.

"You see, they understand respect. You have much to learn."

I've had it with him, I thought. *I'm going back to work.* I gave up waiting for the restoration program to begin, set up a studio in the apartment, and started painting on my own.

Rome was beautiful, but after some months of our first year living abroad, I started having terrible problems walking. I saw Italian and Swiss orthopedists, who found remaining complications from my ski accident. They recommended surgery, but I wanted to be treated by the doctors who had cared for me in the United States. And the beauty of Rome had done little to bring me the happiness I longed for. I suggested to the girls that perhaps we should go back to California, and they were overjoyed. The geographical change had been good for them, but they missed their friends and their country. It was time to go home.

26

School Days of an Art Junky

Back in California, with the kids in school, I had the necessary foot surgery and plunged back into painting. I rented a studio in Venice and opened a contemporary art gallery. But I soon realized I needed to train more seriously to forge the career I wanted, so I started looking into going back to school.

Lee called to invite the kids to his beach house. Even hearing his voice made me feel queasy. We never spoke of his broken promise to come to Italy, much less of his sudden second marriage. Contact with him left me edgy and lonely. Later that day the children came home in tears. Lee's new wife, Pam, had sat them down and shown them an accounting of every penny Lee had spent on them since they had been born. I was furious. I got him on the phone.

"What were you thinking? How could you be so cruel?"

"We just thought they should be aware of the facts," he said.

The issue of money grew uglier. It was not long before I was hauled back into court to alter the terms of my lifetime alimony. The annual amount was to decrease each year, ending completely in several years. It seemed as though greed had destroyed the last of our marital ties. I remembered the young girl I was when I met Lee, planning a music career while working at Rattancraft, not much in the bank. When I fell in love with him, money was the last thing on my mind. It cut deeply that after so many years, money would prove to carve the final dividing line. Any possibility of a friendship with Lee, my great love, the father of my four children, finally vanished.

. His attitude toward me and the children was no longer supportive, and he drew back, less and less present in their lives. Finally, I came across an interview that floored me. Lee referred to us as part of his "past life." When asked about his children, he said that I was a great mother and he had given me full responsibility for them.

Full responsibility. Okay, then I'd better prepare myself to support them. I went back to UCLA and then on to Otis Art Institute. My life was more and more my own.

I first saw Matsumi Kanemitsu, or Mike, as he was affectionately called by those close to him, when he was introduced at the Otis Art Institute student body orientation. We were both in our midforties.

His quiet elegance stood out from the shaggy casualness of the rest of the staff. He was short and slender and immaculately dressed in spotless white duck pants, a pale banana-yellow mandarin over shirt, a faded blue vest, and black velvet Japanese sandals. His thick, long, straight, prematurely silver-gray hair was pulled back into a pony tail, revealing a cherubic oriental face with penetrating eyes and Kewpie doll lips. He held a cigarette between the third and fourth fingers of his raised left hand, and I noticed on his little finger a pearl in a sculpted gold setting. I thought his hands much too beautiful to have ever done a thing but make art. He spoke very little, and I had trouble understanding his broken English, but I was hypnotized by his manner. At the time little did I realize how he would impact my life.

Under his influence I began to see painting in a totally different way. I had essentially been a traditional painter, using many brushes and glazes to produce portraits, still lifes, and landscapes. Though I had moved on to abstract impressionism, I still used outside information to create imagery.

Mike taught me to meditate in order to connect with my subconscious and create from within, then, without hesitation, to release that energy on canvas or paper, many times without brushes, working very wet, letting the painting set up without controlling the outcome. After this I would stop all activity and look at the work for long periods, learning to see where the painting should go, following the discipline of the space and light brought about by color. There was no painstaking copying with a certain goal in mind, but rather a total involvement with the process.

I lost all interest in painting anything that already existed. Thus began my long love affair with abstract expressionism and the master, Kanemitsu. Watching him work, I was fascinated by his initial quiet contemplation, followed by the trancelike dance as he applied paint to a canvas lying flat on the floor. It looked so simple but was really complex—as was Kanemitsu himself.

He was gentle, but powerful, the embodiment of contained passion, the perfect balance of yin and yang. Once he said to me, "I have something for you." He took a nickel from his pocket and, emitting a small grunt, he effortlessly bent the coin in half, handing it to me. He could move polished rocks across the dining table without touching them and penetrate my mind from across a room.

His personal life was difficult. He was born in Utah, the son of Japanese Jewish parents. He was sent to Hiroshima at the age of four to be raised by his traditional grandparents. As a young man, feeling very constrained by the formal, repressive culture in Japan, he left to join Rothko, de Kooning, and Jasper Johns in the abstract expressionist movement in New York. Though his parents were interned during the Second World War, he joined the American army. Following the war he married a beautiful Caucasian actress, causing his wealthy, aristocratic family to disown him. At the height of his success in New York his wife died, and he moved to California to teach. There he married another actress, who eventually abandoned him and their three children.

Together we shared the burden of being single parents. It was a marriage of East and West. We would throw studio parties serving English high tea in a formal Japanese tea ceremony. We regularly had dinners of sushi and sake in downtown Los Angeles and yet would devour hot dogs with the kids at Disneyland. Sometimes we hung out at the racetrack. Mike loved to gamble, like other artists I have known, perhaps because gambling is a natural component of creativity. It's high-risk, grand fun, and addictive. But Mike did not play for small stakes. Poker kept him up and away for days at a time. Whenever we went to the racetrack he always went into the locked room for placing $1,000 minimum bets. I never knew if he won or lost because his expression told me nothing.

On summer break from Otis Art Institute I had a house full of kids, my four and their many friends. The picture had certainly changed since they were young and all living at home.

Christopher had wanted to live at the beach with his dad for the summer, but his stepmother did not welcome him there. He had let his hair grow long and seemed to have little interest in anything but playing the drums. When I tried talking to him about his plans, he just looked at me and smiled. "Don't worry about it, Mama," was his standard reply.

Courtenay, home from the University, of Iowa was moody and ignored me most of the time.

Cynthia and Claudia were still a pleasure to have around. Cynthia was at her adored Courtenay's beck and call. Claudia, jealous of their relationship, spent most of her time on the phone.

"What time did you come in last night?" I asked Christopher when he came down the stairs one noon, disheveled and in a fog. He looked at me and smiled, giving me a hug.

"Mom, I'm not your little boy anymore. Give me a break."

"Well, you're the only little boy I've got. Don't I have the right to know what time you came in?" He took a marijuana cigarette out of his pocket and lit it. "What are you doing?" I asked, dumbfounded.

"Having a little toke before breakfast."

Before I could respond, he sauntered out the back door. Courtenay, Cynthia, and Claudia came in from the beach. I intercepted Courtenay on her way up to shower.

"Courtenay, your brother is out in the garden smoking marijuana."

"So?" she said. "He's been smoking pot since high school. Why are you so upset now?"

"I swear I didn't know."

"Mom, we all were experimenting with pot. I stopped when I went away to college. I got tired of feeling stupid. I guess Christopher enjoys feeling that way."

I was surprised by her candor. She left the room and Cynthia appeared.

"What were you and Courtenay talking about?" she asked.

"About Christopher."

"Did she tell you?"

"She didn't have to. He had the nerve to light up a joint in front of me."

"I'm not talking about Christopher. It's about Courtenay. Anyway, she wanted me to tell you."

"Tell me what?" I said.

"That she's a lesbian."

"Anything else I should know before lunch?" I sat down to catch my breath. "Why didn't she tell me herself?"

"She wasn't sure how you'd take it. She thought you'd be mad."

"Well, I'm not. Just surprised." I had never known Courtenay to be secretive, let alone timid. I went up to her room and knocked. She opened the door, wrapped in a bath towel.

"Can we talk?" I said, sitting on the edge of her bed. "Why didn't you tell me you were gay?"

"I thought you'd be upset. Most of my lesbian friends got hell when their parents found out. Some were thrown out of the house."

"Courtenay, I just want you to be happy. I don't think your life will be easy, but I will always support you." We hugged.

A couple of weeks later I came into the kitchen and found birth control pills on the counter. Cynthia walked in behind me and snatched them up.

"Are these yours? Are you having sex with Josh?"

"No, Mom," she said indignantly. "Josh and I are just friends."

"Well, then who?"

"No one, yet. But I want to and I just want to be ready."

"Oh, Cynthia, please slow down. Promise me you won't rush into sex just out of curiosity."

"Don't worry about it, Mom." She went out the back door.

I was dumbfounded. My perfect children were growing up in ways I had not expected, and I barely recognized them. Right after dinner, I took two aspirin and went to bed, jamming a pillow over my head to block out the Beatles blaring downstairs.

Claudia, now fourteen, out of the blue began to have adolescent rages. One morning she followed me into my bedroom screaming obscenities.

"I don't care about your fuckin' rules! I'm not cleaning my damn room! I am going to the beach!"

"Claudia, please don't be vulgar," I said quietly.

"You think you're so damn perfect. No wonder Dad always got drunk. He probably couldn't stand you if he was sober."

Without answering, I went into my bathroom, turned on the shower, and stepped in, hoping the sound would drown out my daughter's voice. But she was undaunted. Opening the door, she screamed, "I hate you, you bitch! I'm going to Dad's!"

Lee called later. "Claudia wants to live with me. If I'm going to be responsible for her, I want custody. My attorney will draw up the papers."

I talked with Claudia, and she convinced me she wanted to be with her father. Reluctantly, and against my better judgment, I gave in.

I was relieved when that summer was over and everyone, myself included, went back to school.

27

My Studio Life in Venice

I was working on the thesis for my Master of Fine Arts. In the middle of creating an autobiographical installation, the studio I was renting in Venice was sold and I had to find another large space to finish the piece. I passed by an old building on the boardwalk with a "For Sale" sign outside. All my kids had left the nest, so I mortgaged my house for the down payment, then rented it to cover the loan payments. I moved to Venice, created a live-in studio for myself, renovated three other spaces in the building for rental studios, and put in a restaurant for lease.

In front of my studio, 1976

The homeless were hardly noticeable on the west side of Los Angeles in 1976, except in the poor street community of Venice. I had not been aware of this rugged lifestyle, spending most of my time as an adult in the safe, sheltered environment of Santa Monica, never straying too far east of Beverly Hills. I was nervous about moving into this area, but I was in my last year of graduate school and wanted to make art full-time. My alimony would stop completely in two years, and I was actually looking forward to being financially independent.

I knew no one in the Venice area, but was fascinated with the characters on the boardwalk. At sunset I would climb up the ladder from my loft, open the submarine hatch that led to the roof, sit on the deck, have a glass of wine, and watch the street life. A thin, weary, old man with long, gray hair and a beard, dressed in rags, sat on the bench under the gazebo directly below. The gazebo was his home. Every evening before dark he removed a lamp, rug, bedroll, various appliances, and utensils from under the bench to furnish his open space. Of course, there was no electricity and no food to prepare or serve, so the ritual was redundant, but perhaps this daily routine brought him a sense of order and some hope. His mangy German shepherd was always by his side. The local police made a routine weekend sweep of the homeless in the area, picking up the old man on a regular basis. But in a day or two he always returned to his spot.

One afternoon about a month after moving into my studio, sitting up in my safe perch, I noticed the wind had picked up and black clouds were moving onshore. It was only a matter of time before the predicted storm would hit. The old man had a bad cough, and the gazebo offered no shelter against the storm. I climbed down and went out to his spot.

"Hello, I'm Betty, your new neighbor," I said, bending down. He did not look up. His dog's growl stopped me in my tracks and told me to keep my distance. "I came out to invite you in out of the storm," I said timidly. No response. "I'm making a pot of hot chicken stew." I refrained from calling it coq au vin. "You can sleep on the floor of my studio."

After a time he looked up. His low voice was barely audible. "I won't come in without Tim," he said, motioning toward the dog. "And Suzie." He produced a kitten from under his tattered coat.

"That's fine." For a brief moment I wondered if it would be.

When the rain began to fall, the old man ventured into my studio with Tim and Suzie in tow. He looked around carefully, then put his gear down in the corner of the large open space and followed me into the kitchen. I began setting the table. "It's good you came in out of the storm. Sounds like you have a bad cold. Could catch pneumonia." He did not look at me or respond.

"There's a towel by the sink if you want to wash your face and hands." I indicated the bathroom. When he returned there was a noticeable improvement. He took his place at the table and we began the meal in silence. Tim was not much friendlier than his master, staying by him at all times and growling if I came near. I pretended not to notice and poured us each a glass of wine.

"Thanks," he said, not looking up from his plate.

"You're welcome." I was determined to have a conversation. "I just moved here and don't know the area very well."

"I know," he said. So he had been watching me as I had been watching him. He avoided my eyes. "Venice is like a patchwork quilt. We live in the best part, Dudley and Ocean Front Walk. You have to know which streets are safe and those that are not. Don't walk on the Speedway at night. Don't go east of Pacific. Don't go alone between Market and Washington. Those areas are not safe."

"Thanks," I said, surprised by his intelligent response and grateful for the advice. We did not speak again for a while.

He finally looked at me. "Where did you study art?"

"Otis Art Institute."

"Abstract Expressionist, right?"

"That's right," I said, amazed. "Now I'm working in environmental and performance art."

He nodded contemplatively. "That's good. At last art is no longer confined to museums and galleries," he said solemnly. "I believe it's a sign of the times. Artists have an obligation to address real issues, not just make entertaining objects. After all, artists predict the future."

I was delighted by his commentary. Tim, now feeling more relaxed, came over and lay by my feet.

"I've never seen him do that before," the old man said. After dinner he looked at his plate. "That was delicious. I'm sorry I have nothing to give you."

"That's not necessary," I replied. He excused himself and went out the studio door. He returned with a sample pack of Salem cigarettes and handed it to me. Being a smoker at the time I accepted the gift happily and together we smoked all six cigarettes over coffee. After clearing the table, I handed him a towel and a couple of blankets.

"Perhaps a hot bath would be good for your cold," I said. "I'm off to bed." I climbed the stairs to my loft, praying I did not have an ax murderer for a houseguest.

The sun was shining when I awakened the next morning after a sound night's sleep. I peered over the balcony. The old man and Tim were not there. I followed the sound of his kitten and eventually found her downstairs in my photo lab. On the way to my car I took her out to the old man in the gazebo.

"Suzie got stuck in the darkroom," I said matter-of-factly. The old man neither looked up nor spoke. We never spoke to each other after that.

One afternoon I arrived home and found the old man and Tim sitting in front of the door to my studio. When they saw me approaching, they moved back to their regular spot. According to other neighbors, they had positioned themselves there when a gang threatened to break in.

A year later, the police took the old man, Tim, and Suzie away and I never saw them again.

The Christmas holidays were upon us, and Christopher, Courtenay, and Cynthia came to visit me at the studio. Christopher had become a full-time musician and lived in Sonoma. Courtenay had stayed in the Midwest, a political activist working at the Women's Press. Cynthia had given up her plan to be an anthropologist and had returned to her first love, costume design. She was studying at the San Francisco Institute of Design, living in a large Victorian house in Berkeley with four male roommates. She loved the arrangement and they, in turn, loved her. Why not? She was beautiful, could cook, and got along famously with them all.

Sadly, Claudia was missing from the family. Since I had given up all legal custody when she went with her father, I was forbidden to have her with me. She called from a boarding school in northern California asking for help, but unfortunately I could do nothing.

The children didn't care for my studio lifestyle, but we made the best of it, sleeping in my loft, with Christopher and Courtenay in sleeping bags and Cynthia in bed with me.

"Mom," Christopher said the next morning, sounding very paternal, "I don't like you living here. It's not safe."

"I feel perfectly safe," I said. "The street people look out for each other."

"But, Mom, you're not a street person. You have a big studio with a lot of valuable equipment. Remember Woody Allen in one of his first films? He had a record of a growling dog at the door of his apartment. I think you should either get a killer dog or the sound of one."

"Sweetheart, don't worry about it. I'm fine," I said, wondering where I could buy such a record.

My friend Tris finally had his drug habit under control and had become a guru with AA and Narcotics Anonymous. He was looking for a place to hold meetings on Saturday nights, and I offered him the use of my studio. A lively group of drunks and addicts, ranging from bikers to Beverly Hills attorneys, gathered there on a regular basis. Because of the diversity in that street community they fit right in.

Tris dropped by one afternoon just after I had finished my daily tai chi session. Practicing tai chi gave me a sense of both physical strength and emotional calm. It also made me aware of the growing disenchantment I felt with my cumbersome implants.

"Hi, Tris," I said distractedly.

"Did I come at a bad time, Betty?"

"No, it's just"—I grabbed my breasts—"God, these things are so uncomfortable! I don't know what possessed me to get them in the first place. I must have been out of my mind."

"So get rid of them. They have nothing to do with you."

I looked up at him in surprise.

"Having them removed is a completely safe procedure," he said in his best doctor's voice.

"You're right. I don't need them," I said.

The following week they were no more.

28

Flying High and Glad To Be Alive

The sky stretched before me, an endless arc of perfect blue. I could see the fields from an entirely new perspective. I took aerial photographs of the images and carried them from my flights to my studio.

I had learned to fly an airplane and loved being alone and navigating my own course. I had received a BA and MFA in painting and intermedia from Otis and left painting behind for the time being, devoting my time to video, film, and environmental art. I filmed Christo's *Running Fence* project in Petaluma while still in graduate school, then rented out my studio in Venice and moved to Mendocino to design and build a solar structure on the coast overlooking the bay.

Learning to fly was scary, but my first experience of cruising over the Pacific Coast at sunset with a dashing pilot next to me was exciting. After a brief demonstration he gave me the controls, and by the time we landed I was hooked. I purchased the plane, a single-engine Beechcraft Sierra, lessons included. I was a nervous wreck each time I drove to the small airport in Little River for my training. My handsome, charming, ever-present teacher, Roger, helped, but I was still up there in the air.

I was very careful to familiarize myself with the equipment, systems, and controls. I made a thorough exterior inspection each time before entering the airplane, and once inside and before starting the engine, I would adjust and lock the seat belts, turn on the fuel shutoff valve, test and set the brakes, and be sure the electrical equipment was off. With the carburetor cold, mixture rich, throttle one-fourth inch open, master switch on, and propeller area clear, I would start the plane. Then before takeoff I would latch both cabin doors, check flight controls, move tab trim to *Take Off*, set throttle at 1700 RPM, and set flight instruments and radios.

So far, so good. Ready for takeoff. This part always got sticky. Takeoff is always the most dangerous part of flying, and my palms were always wet. Nevertheless, with wing flaps up and throttle full open, I would speed to 70 MPH, lifting the nosewheel at 55. I would then pray a lot while climbing at airspeed of 75-85 MPH with throttle full open, mixture rich. When my prayers were answered and I was safely cruising at 2500 RPM, I was truly in heaven.

I felt very secure handling the controls as long as Roger was next to me. I became a good navigator—"right on the numbers," as they say. It was encouraging to know that precise navigation is the most important quality in a good pilot, as I was convinced I lacked the other requirements, namely courage. I had a secret fear of flying alone and put it off as long as possible even though Roger began to push me.

"It's time, Betty." And then a few weeks later, "Come on, you're more than ready."

"I'll tell you when I'm ready. I want just a few more hours. I don't feel ready." I stalled. There was nothing more to learn as far as the mechanics were concerned, but I was in no way ready emotionally.

I was now in the habit of flying to neighboring airports to practice takeoffs and landings. These maneuvers, called "touch and gos," were a piece of cake as along as Roger was in the cockpit. One day in Ukiah I made a perfect landing and was about to take off again when Roger called out, "See ya later," and jumped out of the plane. I was already taking off and I was alone.

"Shit!" I yelled while the adrenaline surged through my body. In the middle of takeoff at full throttle, with flaps up, at 75 MPH, the passenger door swung open. "Damn you, Roger!" I yelled, leaning over to pull it shut. It was tricky trying to keep my nose up, wings level, and mind focused. "To hell with the door," I mumbled. "Let it fall off." But once I was at cruising level I decided to circle the field a couple of times and correct the problem. After securing the door, I came in for a perfect landing, touching down the main wheels first, lowering the nosewheel slowly, and gently applying the breaks.

I set the parking brake, turned off the equipment, switched off the master switches, and descended from the plane crying, sweating, and swearing. I was glad to be alive. Roger was waiting with open arms and a big smile. After I calmed down, I reluctantly submitted to ruining a perfectly good top in the shirt tail-cutting ceremony which traditionally takes place after one's first solo flight is completed.,

In spite of my early fear of flying alone, I had jumped over a big hurdle. Soon I had enough hours to get my license. I flew a lot in the rural areas, gathering information for field paintings, but never felt secure about coming into major international airports in my little plane. Who wants to get lost on the radar screen?

Once I flew my mother from Mendocino to Santa Rosa for dinner. She was hesitant at first, not about the flying, but about getting in and out of the plane. When we were returning to Mendocino, just the two of us flying through the air, I looked over at her for a moment. So much had passed between us. Before I could say anything, she said, "Just think, I'm up here in the stars, and my daughter is flying the plane."

I felt like Wonder Woman.

My life with Lee seemed very far away. Now twelve years since our divorce, Lee had moved to Tucson, Arizona, with his wife and her children, leaving Claudia behind to be on her own in Lagina Beach, California.

Lee was enmeshed in an ugly lawsuit brought on by Mishell.

One afternoon, I received a phone call from Lee's attorney, Lou Goldman.

"Hi, Betty. How are things going?" he said warmly. This couldn't be the same man who had changed from being a family friend and counselor into a vicious snake during my divorce. Dr. Jekyll, meet Mr. Hyde.

"Hi, Lou, what can I do for you?"

"You know Lee is in a terrible mess. That bitch Mishell is really out to get him."

Despite the fact that that bitch did get him when I lost him and had made my life hell in the process, the hurt and anger I had felt at the time were gone. I felt compassion for Lee and wasn't happy to see him suffering. I'd been following the highly publicized case on TV. Mishell was suing Lee for half the money he had earned while they were together, claiming she had been like a wife during that time. When I saw Lee being interviewed, I felt sad. He had turned into a bitter, cynical man who appeared beaten down by life. Gone was the crazy, fun-loving, passionate guy I had adored.

"How can I help?" I said.

"If we need you to testify, would you be willing to take the stand?"

It took me a moment before I could reply. The idea of being in a courtroom again with Lee made me flinch. But I knew the kids supported him and sensed they'd want me to do whatever I could.

"Yes, Lou. You can count on me."

I never heard from him again and assumed I was not needed for Lee to win the lawsuit.

The case dragged on in the courts for years, and I stopped following it as Lee's name and the newly coined word *palimony* became permanently linked.

Years had passed since we were in touch. I wondered sometimes if our paths were to cross, would he even recognize the woman I'd become? The kids always said that he asked about me, how I was and what I was doing. When they'd report my latest accomplishments, they told me he would turn to anyone in hearing distance and say, "Isn't she amazing?" I could understand how Pam, who had inherited my job of caretaker, had grown to resent me.

Christopher remained protective of his father. At one point he said, "You know, Mom, you never should have divorced Dad. He's been depressed ever since you left him."

"Christopher, honey, please believe me. Your father was depressed long before we separated." As I said those words, the full truth of them hit me. I felt happy I had moved on. Now I could fly a plane. I could own an art gallery. I could paint. I could build homes of my own design. I could do anything.

*   *   *

When Kanemitsu was dying from lung cancer, I went to be with him. I visited him regularly and sadly watched him waste away. He didn't give up smoking until the oxygen mask got in the way. He lay on the sofa, barely able to speak, helping his staff curate years of work for posterity. Those visits were difficult for me, but he always insisted that I bring new work to discuss. As he slowly disappeared, I felt like the student being abandoned by the teacher. Sensing my pain, he took my hand and said, "Don't worry, dear Betty, you know how to paint."

Since then his spirit has always been with me in my studio, his art fills my home, and his love fills my heart. Ours was a bittersweet journey.

At the Matsumi Kanemitsu Retrospective in Kyoto, Japan 1998

*   *   *

29

Family Wedding Bring Back Memories of Divorce

For almost a month I'd been on the phone daily with Cynthia. She was living in San Francisco with her boyfriend, Edward, and she was pregnant. No matter how many times we went through it, she couldn't seem to land on the right decision: she could have the baby and marry Edward; have the baby and not marry him; or not have the baby and not marry, even though she loved Edward. She swung back and forth between panic and reason. I listened, amazed at the choices available to my twenty-five-year-old daughter in 1981. Almost thirty years before I had been in her exact shoes, single, pregnant, and in love. I knew only one option: to marry the father and have the baby.

When Cynthia called, three months into her pregnancy, to tell me she had finally decided to have the baby and marry Edward, I shelved whatever mixed feelings I had. And when I heard, "I need you, Mom," I was on my way.

This wasn't what I had dreamed of for my daughter. Edward was bright, handsome, and charming; but he was a drummer in a rock-and-roll band, just getting by. He wasn't in any position to take on a wife and child. But Cynthia had made her decision, and in the next few days I stored my few possessions in a friend's garage, packed a few necessities, including a ten-year-old sea-green silk dress suitable for mother of the bride, and drove to San Francisco. It was time to plan a wedding.

Cynthia was an old-fashioned girl at heart. She sewed an ivory silk-satin renaissance gown of her own design, covered with imported lace and hand-sewn seed pearls, to wear for the occasion. The empire waist was perfect for a pregnant bride.

She called Lee to tell him the news. I didn't push for many details of the call, but gathered that her father, while taken aback at the news he was about to become a grandfather, agreed to pick up the tab. I wondered if Cynthia could see my relief. Times had become increasingly rough in Los Angeles. Happy not to have to stress over the wedding budget, I leased the elegant, old Victorian Casa Madrona overlooking the bay in Sausalito. We planned a midday wedding, including a sit-down luncheon followed by dancing to a live band, and I sent out a hundred shell-pink invitations with embossed flowers on the border.

I was so involved with the guest list, menu, flowers, and music that I pushed away the thought of spending the afternoon with Lee. We had rarely spoken in ten years. He was remarried to a woman with four children of her own who was very resentful of his first family.

In planning the seating, I arranged a special table for the families of the bride and groom. Edward's parents were our family's mirror opposite, having been married forever, surrounded by devoted sisters, brothers, sons, and daughters, all arriving en masse to celebrate the wedding. How would my daughter feel facing her new picture-perfect in-laws surrounded by her alcoholic movie-star father, hostile stepmother, free-spirited older brother, militant lesbian older sister, and high school dropout younger sister, not to mention a mother, who, in spite of years of therapy, was still a bit of a mess?

I shuddered and decided to give my place at the wedding table to Lee's wife. *It will be easier for Cynthia*, I thought, but deep down I was sparing myself the disapproving glances of the in-laws and the embarrassing remarks of my ex-husband, particularly if he drank too many toasts to the bride and groom.

But none of that happened. In fact, it was a perfect wedding. The sight of Cynthia, in her beautiful gown, on Lee's arm, descending the carved mahogany stairs to the familiar Mendelssohn performed by my aunt Rella, filled my heart. The simple service, followed by loving champagne toasts and a delicious lunch while overlooking the sunlit bay, was flawless. The dancing was fun, even with the father of the bride, who behaved himself in every way. After having endless family photos taken posed to look as though Lee and I would be together till death did us part, he and his wife made a hasty departure. The bride and groom went off happily on their honeymoon, and family and friends drifted away. Fait accompli.

Cynthia's wedding day, with Christopher, Courtenay, Lee, myself, and Claudia, 1982

Alone that evening, I fought spiraling downward. Nothing like a wonderful wedding to emphasize the heartbreak of divorce. It had been years since I had been with Lee, and I fought any feelings of sadness, betrayal, or anger.

After the wedding I moved to San Francisco and promised Cynthia I would be on hand for the birth of her baby. I picked up catering jobs to pay the rent, determined to save my only asset, the Venice building. My daughter was doing just fine, working in the costume department of the San Francisco Opera Company up until her due date, and it felt good to be nearby, helping her get ready for the birth of her first child.

30

Paris Revisited: My Second Home

Following the arrival of my grandson, Matthew, I was summoned to Paris. A producer friend had moved there with his wife and three children for a change of scene, had become bored, and asked me to think of a business venture for him.

"Why don't you open an American bar and grill?" I suggested. "You know about good food, and Parisians love everything American. Open a restaurant that features American food—you know, an oyster bar, hamburgers, steaks, apple pie. Have good American art on the walls. Show living American artists like Diebenkorn and Rauschenberg. What about a Red Grooms installation? Have live jazz on Sunday afternoons. Got the picture?"

"Brilliant," he said. "I'm going to do it. I want you to come over and put it together."

"Whoa, I don't want to be in the restaurant business."

"You don't have to be in the restaurant business. I want you to design the restaurant. It's your idea, and I want you to create everything you talked about. I'll raise the money and run the business."

At my attorney's insistence, we drew up a simple contract, giving me a small percentage of the gross profits after the restaurant opened. I packed and kissed my family good-bye.

Living in Paris in the eighties was very different from what I had known in the sixties, when I used to hang out at the Hôtel de Crillon, mingling with the top designers of the fashion world and bringing back their latest collections to sell in my boutique on Rodeo Drive. Instead, I was residing in a modest, five-floor walk-up in a fourteenth-century building in Le Marais near the Seine, a struggling artist designing a restaurant.

The flat consisted of two large rooms with French doors, high ceilings, and oversized French windows facing Rue de Pont Luis Phillip. The entry led to the salon, and off to the right was a small kitchen. I had converted the second room beyond the salon into my studio and bedroom, with an adjoining bathroom.

"Hi, baby," my producer friend greeted me as I arrived at the potential site for our project.

"Perfect location for an American bar and grill, don't you think?" I said. "Franklin Delano Roosevelt Boulevard?"

"Heaven-sent," he said. "What about the Wilsons? They interested in investing?"

"Maybe. I didn't pursue it. I'm not good at asking for money. That's your department."

"Okay, but they're your friends."

"That's the point. I don't like soliciting my friends."

He looked disappointed. "Why? I don't understand."

"I guess you wouldn't. You're a producer."

After that he began to exclude me from the project.

Before I knew it the Christmas season was upon me. I had mixed feelings about being away from home at this time of year despite the beauty of the city. During the holidays the twinkling trees running the length of the Champs-Élysées were magical. This year, to add to the elegance, the city had suspended life-size antique cars above Rue Royale. I was lonely and missed my family and friends more than usual, so I made it a habit to walk up and down the boulevards at dusk to watch the special lights come on and enjoy the windows.

One afternoon, after the rain, I changed out of my jeans and sweatshirt, put on a heavy, grey tweed coat and black high boots, and set out for my stroll. I grabbed my favorite gray silk umbrella—a leftover gift from Lee—on my way out the door since the winter weather was at best unpredictable. The brisk, damp air of winter by the Seine felt wonderful on my skin as I walked along Rue de Rivoli. I liked the way I looked and felt when living in Paris. Walking miles each day in the city as well as working out at the gym kept me ten pounds lighter than my car-driving lifestyle in California.

Before I realized it I had walked from Isle St. Louis, through the Tuilleries, past the Louvre, and all the way to the seventh arrondissement, a distance of about thirty blocks. I turned into Place de la Concorde and headed toward the Ritz. I didn't want to miss the hotel's beautiful windows full of animated, life-size figures acting out a Christmas scene.

I stood there taking in the surreal beauty of the performance for some time. When I glanced in the window to the right, I saw the reflection of an older woman standing near me. I looked away, thinking to myself, *She's American*, a safe guess since there were about fifty thousand Americans living in Paris and the Ritz was one of their hangouts. A moment later I glanced over again and realized I had been looking at my own image. *This couldn't possibly be me*, I thought. *Yes, it is*, my inner self countered. I had no idea I looked that old, however "that old" looks. *Well, this is the way my age looks on me*, I told myself. Funny, I never seem to look old to me when I deliberately look at myself in the mirror.

Continuing to stare at myself with great curiosity, I laughed, remembering a woman friend telling me that one day we would become our mothers. I hoped not. My mother and I were nothing alike. Or were we? I looked nothing like her, at least. She was five foot six. I was almost five foot eleven. She was heavyset and had dark hair, and I had always been slender and fair. And when it came to behavior, we were exact opposites. She was quite helpless and had no ambition. I was probably too independent for my own good and had always set my sights high. My mother used to drive me crazy because she could never make a decision, right or wrong. How could she sit all morning in her housecoat drinking coffee? She never had a plan to do anything. I didn't remember her ever taking me anywhere—to a movie, out to lunch, not even for a walk. Certainly not a ride, because she didn't drive. She always depended on someone else, and for some reason there was always someone to take charge. No wonder I was so determined to make choices and welcome change.

The shock of that reflection and the flood of feelings it brought put me in touch with my own mortality. I went back to my flat, called Air France, and made a reservation to fly home to spend the holidays with my children.

I spent a happy Christmas with family and friends, getting acquainted with my grandson.

"Has Lee seen Matthew?" I asked Cynthia after the first couple of days.

"He stopped by once for a few minutes," she said and turned her attention to the baby.

I called Daddy. Faye answered the phone.

"I'll call your father. He'll be so happy to hear from you. He's not feeling so well."

"Is that my little girl?" Daddy's voice was weak but still had the old charm.

"Hi, Daddy."

"What've you been up to? Still traveling all over the world?"

"I flew in from Paris to see my kids for Christmas."

"Well, when are you going to see your daddy?"

"I thought I would take the train down and we could celebrate New Year's Eve together."

I could hear my father's spirits lifting.

"That would be terrific, kiddo. Daddy will show you a good time."

It had been some years since I had seen Daddy, and I didn't know quite what to expect. Faye met me at the station. She had put on a great deal of weight but still had the yellow, bleached hair and was as sweet as ever. I was shocked when I walked into the living room of their modest ranch house sitting in the middle of a dying avocado grove. The paint-peeled walls of the shabby living room were covered with Lee Marvin posters, and terry towels partially hid the worn patches of an old, green upholstered sofa. A tired-looking, eighty-two-year-old man sat in a leather recliner, feet extended, legs wrapped in bandages. He was watching a John Wayne Western on the television. It was hard to believe this was the same person I had first seen wearing silk pajamas in the master suite of a Mediterranean mansion.

He finally looked up and gave me a smile. "Hi, kiddo."

I went over and gave him a quick kiss. "Hi, Daddy."

"Well, I better get ready so we can celebrate the New Year." He pulled himself up and shuffled out of the room.

"Your father's having trouble with his legs," Faye said. "It was sweet of you to come."

My father came out of his bedroom wearing an Hawaiian shirt. He asked Faye to get out the Lincoln. She went to the garage, reappeared in a fancy, black-and-silver sedan, and drove us to his favorite watering hole for dinner. He introduced me to the locals.

"I want you to meet my daughter, Lee's wife."

I smiled at the introduction. At least I was no longer being passed off as his niece. Daddy ordered a glass of wine for me, a Coke for Faye, and a scotch and milk for himself.

"Daddy, you know Lee and I have been divorced for years," I murmured to him gently as we moved away from his crowd.

"C'mon, kiddo, don't be so serious. Let's just have a good time." He was ready for a second drink, and his eyes were getting that old, familiar glaze. The small amount of booze he had consumed was working much faster in old age. When he began to slur his words, I knew it was time to get out of there and announced I had to catch the train back to Los Angeles. He wished me a happy new year and stayed behind to have another drink with his cronies while Faye drove me to the station. I greeted the New Year with my fellow passengers on a sad train ride back to Los Angeles.

My last visit with Daddy and Faye 1986

I waited until I had recovered from that experience and then drove to Oregon to visit my eighty-year-old mother. I left at dawn and arrived in time for dinner. The next morning she was sitting at the Formica table in the kitchen, sipping her second cup of coffee. She looked particularly frail in her blue flannel robe, compared with my last sight of her a year before.

I sat facing her in my jeans and sweatshirt, finishing my tea and toast. "Mother, I'm trying to put together some pieces of my life. I need your help."

"Oh, Betty, let's not get into that." She looked trapped, twisting the tissue in her hand.

I was not about to back down. "Okay. I can come here every year and we can talk about the weather, your garden, and any topic that's safe. Or we can get to know each other. I have so many questions. Please help me."

She pulled herself up straight, avoiding my eyes. "What do you want to know?"

I wanted to avoid causing her more pain but pushed on. "Is it true my father wanted a divorce and, instead of discussing it with you, he asked his mother to break the news?"

My mother stared at the table as if she had not heard me, then sighed. "Who told you that?" She paused. "It was either Grandma Ebeling or Aunt Rella." She paused again. "Yes, Grandma Ebeling was the one who told me," she sighed.

"Didn't that upset you?" I asked tenderly.

"I don't know. I don't remember. Anna Ebeling felt I wasn't good enough for her son. I guess I was relieved when it was over. Ernie wasn't exactly a devoted husband, you know. He drank and played around."

"That must have been hurtful," I said, remembering the anguish caused by my own deceitful husband. "It sounds like he was not good enough for you."

My mother looked at me, tears in her eyes. That was the first time she had ever spoken to me of my father.

"Mother, I don't want to make you sad, but I need to know what happened. Is it true Aunt Rella wanted to adopt me?"

"Yes," my mother whispered, avoiding my eyes. "But I didn't want her to have you. You were my baby."

That sounded strange. I had never felt like her baby. I let it go. "I know in my heart you love me," I said.

"I've always loved you."

"Then how could you leave Dick and me?"

Her sudden look of anguish made me want to take back my words, but it was too late. I was on a mission.

"I'm sorry," she moaned. "I know I did a terrible thing, but I didn't know what else to do. I needed to get married and have someone take care of me."

I wanted to tell her my brother and I had needed a mother to take care of us, but I did not want to hurt her more. We all had suffered enough. At that moment I forgave her for abandoning me when I was a child. She had done the best she could.

Our talks during that visit brought about a wonderful change. She seemed, for the first time, to be completely comfortable with me, and I with her.

My visit with Mother 1986

Leaving Los Angeles after an eighty-degree Christmas break in 1986, I dreaded returning to the damp cold of Paris. Nobody would ever move there for the climate. To be practical, I took my shabby mink coat out of its hiding place in the back of my storage closet and brought it along for warmth. After the pure torture of a crowded, non-stop, ten-hour coach flight, I arrived home to a freezing flat. I dragged my computer and luggage up the bare oak circular staircase, reached the door, and was trying to get the key into the lock with my gloved hand when the computer slipped back down the waxed stairs all the way to the third floor. I was tempted to leave it there, but went back down, brought it up, finally opened the door, and went in.

The heat had been off for a month. When the cold air hit me, I was happy to keep on the old mink while I opened the closet door to light the pilot in the antiquated heater. Once the chill was off, I hung the coat on a hook in the entry and stumbled through the salon into the back studio, closing the French doors behind me. I dropped my clothes on the floor, slipped into a nightgown, and soon fell into the deep sleep of exhaustion.

Some time later I awakened slightly, rose as if in a dream, and mechanically made my way to the studio door. I tried to open it, but it was stuck. What was wrong? It couldn't be locked. Alert now, I used all my strength and finally was able to pull the door toward me. I was overwhelmed by the heat and flames coming from the hall. I stood there, hypnotized.

Then it hit me—*fire!* I was five floors up with no outside stairs—no escape! The only way out was through that burning hallway. I began to cough from the smoke, realized I had no way to reach the kitchen for water, opened the windows to get some air, saw at once I was probably feeding the fire with added oxygen, and closed the windows. I ran back through the studio into the bathroom, wet a towel to cover my face, and returned to the fire. I fought the dreaded feeling of helplessness, trying to figure a way to make it through the hall to the only exit.

At that moment the mink miraculously fell off the hook onto the floor, making a narrow path. I seized the opportunity and ran over the fur, dragging it out behind me. I found myself on the landing, a trembling, smoke-covered figure in my formerly shell pink turned smudged-gray nightgown. I covered the gown with my coat.

I tried hopelessly to remember the French word for *fire*, but my adopted language had left me completely. I finally yelled, "Help!" and my neighbors came from the floor below. I sat in a trance on the stairs, wrapped in the stench of a burned animal while the neighbors called the fire department and brought in an extinguisher to contain the blaze.

Finally the nightmare was over, except for the smoke and my shattered nerves.

The next day I discovered the cause of the fire. The landlady, doing some touchup while I was away, had left a can of paint thinner in the closet next to the heater. The coat, unwearable in its altered state, had saved my life and finally had become a prized possession.

The months passed. I rarely heard from the producer and I came to realize that he, who I thought was my friend, had no intention of honoring our contract. He was using my ideas and freezing me out in the process. I had been betrayed, with no connections to force the issue and no green card, a necessity for earning a legal income in Paris. I confronted him.

"Why did you insist you needed me for this project? I came over here, researched locations, designed the restaurant, introduced you to perspective investors, and you shut me out."

"It just turned out differently than I planned."

"Why did you string me along? You didn't even have the decency to tell me my services were not needed. After all, I gave you the idea."

"Yes, Betty, I know it was your idea. But it was just an idea."

"You producers always seem to forget that without other people's ideas you would be without a job." I got up and stormed out.

I packed up and moved back to Los Angeles.

After returning to L.A., I went back to my first love—painting. But after ten years in intermedia, my paintings were conceptual in content, rather than simply for decoration or entertainment.

A couple of years later I was deeply saddened by the news that Jerry Rogers was dying from AIDS. It was heartbreaking to see him waste away from the handsome, talented man I had loved to a walking ghost. I was with him at the end when he was taken away with morphine. During that time I participated in sad farewells to several other talented gay artist friends. Each death seemed so terribly unfair and left permanent gaps in my life.

In August, 1987, after attending the Joseph Beuys retrospective in Germany, I returned to the flat I had rented in Paris for August. I was barely in the door when the phone rang. It was my neighbor. "Betty?"

"Yes. How are you, Maggie?" I asked. "Just got in. The train was late."

"Are you all right?"

"Tired, but it was a good trip. The retrospective in Cologne was wonderful and Berlin is fascinating. Wonderful art scene. Much more sophisticated than the rest of the country."

She did not respond. Finally she said, "Don't you know?" She sounded strange.

"What do you mean? Know what?" I sat down.

"Oh. I thought you would have heard. I saw the news on TV. I'm sorry to tell you, but Lee died."

"Oh, my God," I said. A pain shot through my heart. I didn't know I still cared, but he was the love of my life, for better or worse, and the father of my children. "Thanks for telling me. I'm all right. I've got to hang up and call the kids. I'll get the next flight home."

When I arrived in Los Angeles all four kids were there to meet me. We hugged and cried. Adding to their sadness, the children were not invited to their father's home for the private funeral service. To make up for that final rejection, we had a special memorial for Lee at Nancy and Carroll O'Connor's home on the beach and invited all the friends from our marriage days. The children and I each chose a special poem, which we read in Lee's honor. Then all of us sang his favorite hymn, "Amazing Grace," as we walked to the water's edge with hearts full of love and arms full of roses. We threw the flowers into the sea.

A few months later we learned, except for a $10,000 insurance policy, our kids had been cut out of their father's will. His widow would not even allow them to retrieve the gifts they had given him over the years. It broke my heart to learn that Lee had been able to forget his own children and leave everything to his second wife and her kids. This was not the man I had known and loved.

31

Homeless: A Test in Courage

While I was figuring out my next move, a hotshot real estate developer seduced me into selling my only asset, the Venice Beach building, for what seemed like a fortune. I had rented my studio in 1980 and, because of the homeless and drug scene, had not lived there for some time. I spent months with brokers and attorneys who talked way over my head about making a tax-deferred exchange by putting me into another real estate investment. They promised me the purchase of the three-million-dollar building full of wealthy tenants in San Luis Obispo would make me really rich.

Greed got the best of me. I saw myself as a land baroness, living without a financial care in the world, spending the rest of my life making art and traveling first-class to exotic places. I would finally be on easy street. Also I would be able to give the children $50,000 each as down payment on a home of their own. I thought this would help to make up for their father's negligence.

I was celebrating the close of escrow at Two Bunch Palms in Desert Hot Springs, having a much-needed rest. It was easy to imagine my life of luxury had already begun as I floated contentedly in the warm mineral pool, one life preserver around my neck to support my head and another around my ankles. My biggest challenge that day was keeping my paperback above water while trying to stay awake until my massage appointment. An attendant appeared and signaled that I had a phone call. *What a drag,* I thought, but I thanked him, reluctantly crawled out of my luxurious haven, and grabbed a towel. The desert air suddenly felt cold on my skin as I put on my terry cloth robe and slippers, making my way down the path to my room. I picked up the phone.

"Is this Betty Marvin?" I did not recognize the warm, friendly voice.

"Yes. Who is this?"

"This is Clifford Branch. We don't know each other. Sorry to disturb you, but I felt I had to call you."

"I don't understand. How did you get this number?"

"I called your house in Ventura and spoke with your daughter."

For God's sake, I thought. *Who is this guy, a complete stranger, calling me?* He seemed to be talking too fast, and his voice kept fading in and out. I heard him mention the name of the man I'd bought the new building from, but I was so disoriented his words made no sense. I didn't come to until I heard the words *fraud* and *con artist.*

"What are you talking about, Mr. . . . ? Sorry, I didn't get your name."

"Clifford Branch."

"Well, Mr. Branch, I pray this is some kind of a joke."

"No, Mrs. Marvin. Honestly, I wish it were. I live in San Luis Obispo, and I've had my own dealings with Richard Witherspoon, the previous owner of the building you purchased. He approached me over a year ago to buy the same building. I had a private detective check him out and found his financial statement showing three million dollars in assets was false."

I closed my eyes as Mr. Branch went on. *This isn't happening,* I thought. *It's like I'm in some old crime movie.*

"When I heard you had bought the place, I felt I had to call you. Witherspoon was already close to bankruptcy last year. I reported him to the police, but I heard he's already left the state."

I was in shock. "There must be some mistake. I had a real estate attorney, a tax accountant, and two commercial brokers working on this deal for one year. They put the contract together. I didn't simply buy a building. I bought it with all the leases and Mr. Witherspoon himself staying on as the anchor tenant." I paused as the truth sank in. "Why didn't you contact me before I signed the escrow papers?"

"I'm sorry," he said. "I didn't know you'd bought the building until yesterday. I tracked you down as fast as I could. I wish . . ." He fumbled for the right words. "I wish I'd been there in time. I'm sure you're a nice woman."

Nice, I thought, *nice and naïve.* I had played with the big boys, the sharks, and got screwed.

191

"Thank you. I don't know what to say. I have to get my bearings. I don't know what to do."

"I'll help you any way I can," he said. "Take my phone number. If you come up, I'll show you my files. My friend is a top litigation attorney here in town. If you want, I'll arrange for him to meet with you."

I needed to get off the phone to think. I took Mr. Branch's number, thanked him again, hung up the phone, and just stood there, replaying the conversation in my head. If he was telling me the truth, I'd lost everything with the stroke of a pen. I lay down on the bed and watched the ceiling circle above me.

The next day I drove to San Luis Obispo, met with Mr. Branch, and then with the attorney who took my case on contingency.

In the meantime things were quickly falling apart around me. I had to sell my house to get my hands on some money. But it was 1991, the real estate market was in the toilet, and I was batting zero with buyers, even at a low asking price. I finally struck a deal with a young couple who were short on cash themselves: they'd buy half the house and pay for the other half in three years. My Social Security would just cover the rest of the mortgage, but I'd have to move out.

I arranged a quick art sale for some fast cash. I would sell all my equipment, my jazz records, and books. It was hard to let them go. Surrounded by packing boxes, I opened a bottle of wine to keep myself going. *When in doubt, throw it out,* I told myself, taking things down from the shelves to put into storage, take to the kids for safekeeping, or give to Goodwill. I kept the phone on as long as I could to stay in touch with friends and family, but just before I moved out it was cut off, so I kept the TV on for company.

While packing up the kitchen, my attention was caught by a TV documentary on three middle-aged homeless women. I stopped what I was doing and stood among my packing boxes watching. One woman had been married to an attorney and had resided in Bel Air. She lost everything in a divorce settlement and was sleeping in her car parked near her old address. During the day she hung around her favorite department store, Neiman Marcus, checking out free makeup and sneaking into the bathroom to use the facilities. *Oh, my God, I could never live that way,* I thought. The fates had been even more unkind to the other two women profiled, one of whom had become a street person. When I heard the narrator say that most Americans were two paychecks away from being homeless, I looked around me, thought back to my homeless neighbor in Venice, and shuddered.

"I'll be fine," I told my daughter Cynthia as I was leaving, trying to sound upbeat. "I'll be at Willy's. Don't worry about me."

Willy had been a long-loved friend from my Malibu days who drowned while diving in the Caribbean the year before. His California ranch house stood empty. Knowing my circumstances and how close Willy and I had been, his daughter, Stephanie, contacted me about the possibility of my staying there temporarily. "He'd want you in his house," she told me. We worked out an agreement in which I'd fix up the place so she could eventually rent it. I was lucky. I had somewhere to go while I got my bearings.

I called Christopher. "What shall I do with Sadie?" I had adopted my German Shepherd after returning from Paris and moving into the Ventura home.

"Keep her with you. Wherever you are, she will be your support and protector."

So I drove down Highway 101 to Willy's house in Malibu with my German Shepherd by my side and my few belongings packed into the trunk of my old Chrysler convertible.

I unlocked the front door and, with some trepidation, went in. Things were as he had left them—in a mess. Willy never really cared about the place and hadn't bothered to make it a real home. It was sort of a rest stop between traveling adventures, a bachelor's hideout with a bed, bureau, stove, refrigerator, dining table and chairs, reading chair and lamp, globe, and atlas. The living room was cluttered with stacks of travel brochures, copies of *National Geographic*, old pipes, and broken sunglasses. The Hermes cologne I had given him for his trip was left sitting on the lamp table. He used the dining table to hold his toy train with surrounding village and landscape. Looking at the toy train brought tears to my eyes. I hadn't been in Willy's house since his death.

I went into the kitchen, opened a bottle of cheap Chardonnay, and went out on the terrace. The house was on the wrong side of the highway, overlooking the multi-million—dollar mansions side by side on the beach. A long time ago one of those houses had been mine, a 10,000-square-foot Mediterranean. It felt surreal to be standing there, a temporary tenant of Willy's ramshackle house, remembering my past in Malibu. Somewhere I still had the key to the private beach club. Watching the waves roll in, I knew I'd never use the key. My old friends wouldn't want to see me down and out. Their idea of hard times was to drive the Mercedes rather than call for the limo.

Over the next few weeks, I removed Willy's personal belongings, cleaned, painted, and replanted the garden. Finally, the place looked habitable; better than that, it looked like a home. The house was ready for lease. When it rented it would be time for me to move on, but where?

People started coming to see the house. I heard from Stephanie only a few days later.

"Betty, honestly, what you did with Dad's house is a miracle. I can't thank you enough."

"Thank you. It's been wonderful to be here."

"The . . ."She paused. "The tenants I've accepted are pretty much ready to move in as soon as I give them the word."

Right, I thought. *It's time to go.*

"Betty?" Stephanie's voice broke through, "is that okay? Like, if we say, next weekend?"

"Next weekend is fine. I promise I'll be long gone and the house will be ready and waiting."

I left the house as promised. Sadie and I drove down the road to Ventura in search of a job and a place to sleep. The day was bright and might have felt full of possibility when I was younger. But driving with no destination at sixty-six years old, I was trying not to panic, hoping to wrest out what opportunities I could summon for myself. Before leaving my house, I'd sent out dozens of resumes, answering any classified ad I thought might be even a slight possibility. Three college degrees should have made me eligible for something. But my age was against me. Not one business called.

I stopped to rest in Arroyo Verde Park, letting Sadie have a run while I tried to figure out my next move. Two barking, white, miniature poodles raced across the park to stage an attack. A short, fat, brunette in her forties followed behind yelling, "Goddamn it! Shut up and get back here, you little bastards." The dogs ignored her and Sadie ignored them. The woman plopped down next to me, lit a cigarette, and gave me the once-over. "You look like you just lost your best friend," she said, taking a swig from a brown paper bag. "Carrot juice," she explained.

I smiled and wished she'd go away.

"Park's great for dogs. You bring yours here a lot?"

"No, just today."

"You visiting?"

Please, please, I thought, *I'm in no mood for a conversation.*

"I'm Millicent. I live a few blocks from here." She pointed vaguely. "How 'bout you?"

I don't know what made me tell her what I'd kept secret from friends. "Actually, Millicent, I have nowhere to go. I need a place to stay and a job, and I need them today." Just saying it out loud made me feel queasy.

"Huh," said Millicent, lighting a fresh cigarette from the butt of the other. "You just might be in luck. My roomie moved out Tuesday."

I couldn't imagine myself as Millicent's "roomie," but I followed her car to a modest stucco house nearby, beige and brown, inside and out. She talked nonstop as she showed me through. "You have your own bath and private entrance. Use the kitchen anytime. I never use it. Hardly ever home. I'm a vegetarian. Strict. Mostly carrot juice and wheatgrass." She took a deep drag on her cigarette. "Four hundred bucks a month. Now that's a good deal, huh? What do you say?"

"I'll take it," I said impulsively. I had no idea how I'd pay the rent, but I had to live somewhere, and if this was not a perfect arrangement, at least there was a kitchen. Catering? I'd figure out something to provide enough cash income to survive.

"So go get your stuff," Millicent said in a bossy tone.

"It's all in the trunk of my car," I told her. I went out to retrieve a bag of clothes and my typewriter. I had sold my computer. When I came into the chaotic kitchen, Millicent was cleaning out a couple of cupboards. A flat of wheatgrass was growing on the counter. The sink was full of yellow-stained glasses and coffee mugs, brown with soggy cigarette butts. "There you are," she said. I scrubbed these out just for you." She opened the refrigerator and moved a mound of aged organic carrots. "You can have this shelf." She took out a carton of milk, read the date, smelled it, made a face, and poured it into the sink as I stood there mute, trying not to laugh. Boy, I knew how to pick 'em.

"I got yoga—damn, I'm late—so I'll see ya later, 'kay?" Before I could say anything, Millicent was running out the door.

Sadie padded up and nuzzled me.

"Well, baby," I told her, "it's just for a while."

What little money I had left from my Social Security check went into the first month's rent, leaving just enough for me to buy supplies and make use of the kitchen. That afternoon I went to Kinko's and printed up flyers announcing "Sadie's Basket: A Gourmet Luncheon Delivery Service."

The next morning I was up at 5:30 making sandwiches, packaging salads, desserts and cold drinks, and organizing napkins, plastic cups, spoons, and forks. I loaded the car and at 10:30, dressed in white jeans, shirt, and red-striped apron, made the first stop on my mapped-out route, a building of law offices. I could barely bring myself to go in. *It's just acting,* I told myself in the elevator. *Say your lines and you'll do fine.*

"Good morning! Sadie's Basket is here, full of tasty treats—organic, homemade, and delicious." I was standing in front of a receptionist, all of nineteen, giving me a puzzled look as I handed her a flyer.

She gave it a quick glance and buzzed the offices. "Anyone need lunch? There's some woman out here selling food." Doors opened, and it was like a storm hit. Within ten minutes the reception area was full of hungry attorneys, paralegals, and secretaries who bought everything in sight and sent me back to the car for more. After gathering up the cash and assuring the office I would return every day at the same time, I was off to the next address, an office building of doctors and dentists, followed by a hairdressing salon and spa. I refilled the baskets, gave myself a pep talk, and each time sold out.

I lay on my bed that evening counting the money I had left after hitting the market for the next day's supplies. The door suddenly swung open with a bang.

"Where the hell's my juicer?" Millicent lurched into my bedroom wearing nothing but panties that had seen better days and holding a bottle of Bud.

"I can't find a fuckin' thing in my own kitchen!" She turned and staggered out, shouting over her shoulder. "My phone's been ringin' off the hook! Someone named Cynthia! Call her back and tell her to knock it off!"

I got up and locked my door, then called my daughter. "Cynthia, this lady's not wrapped too tight. Better not phone here. I'll call you."

"Mom, you'd better move."

"Not right now. Soon, I promise."

Cynthia came the next afternoon to check out my new residence.

"Some spread," she teased me lightly.

Millicent burst through the door, her hands full of parking citations. "Look at these fuckin' tickets, will ya?" She threw them on the table.

"Where do they expect you to park in this damned city? I get back to my car and that fuckin' meter maid is writing up another one. Two in one day! I almost belted that bitch. I've gotta have some wheatgrass." She went to the refrigerator, pulled out a jug of vile green liquid, and took a gulp. Cynthia kissed me softly on the cheek and slipped out. Millicent didn't seem to notice she'd ever been there.

My lunchtime business was at least helping me hang on. Over the next three months my door-to-door deliveries tripled while I lost fifteen pounds. But God, the cost to my spirit! Not since my waitressing days in college had I found a job so demeaning.

One day a secretary lingered over the basket. "How come you never have the veggie gourmet left?"

"You're always the last person to come out," I told her. We'd had this dialogue almost every day for a week. She turned her back and engaged in conversation with a coworker. After a minute I interrupted, "Would you like something else?"

She glared at me. "Just wait. Can't you see I'm busy?"

"Well, I have other appointments. I have to go."

"So, go then!"

I started to leave then turned back. "Please tell your coworkers I won't be servicing this office any-more."

She stared at me open-mouthed as I walked out.

I finally let my curiosity get the best of me and peeked into Millicent's room while she was out. It was like stepping into a frat boy's pad. Worse. The stench of empty beer bottles and cigarette butts almost knocked me over. Filthy clothes were crumpled on the floor, newspapers were spread out on the unmade bed, and half-empty cartons of Chinese food were everywhere.

I closed her door and took a really long, hot shower, knowing I had to get out of there.

Millicent got worse. I found hand-cut holes in my sheets just after she'd asked me if I knew what had happened to her scissors. Some afternoons I knew she'd been in my room—I could smell the stale smoke, her body odor. I was looking at roommate ads and counting the days until I could move out. When my phone rang, I hoped it was someone calling about a room.

"Hello?"

"Yeah, is this the Basket?"

"I beg your pardon?"

"Basket! Basket! *Comida!*"

"Oh, yes." I reached for a pen. "Would you like to place an order?"

"You got nerve, bitch," the woman's voice said to me. I had no idea who she was. I started to hang up but she was fast. "I got a catering truck, been here five years. You're in my territory. You don't have a license, and I'm gonna report you. *Comprendez,* bitch?" She slammed down the phone.

The next day I discovered the cord on my phone had been cut. That did it. It was time to shut down the business and get out of Dodge. I left Millicent half a month's rent on top of the juicer.

With a little discipline and a lot of faith, I made it through that first year without sleeping in my car, going on welfare, borrowing money, or taking charity. I catered dinner parties in return for a night's stay here and there with friends. I pulled out all the domestic skills that mothers never get paid for—cooking, gardening, cleaning, recovering pieces of furniture—anything I could think of in exchange for a few nights' stay or a chunk of change. When I was lucky, I got house-sitting gigs. Sadie and I drove throughout California, going wherever work took me, to receive room and board, often from friends and acquaintances, in exchange for services rendered.

One job found me serving canapés at a tea party not far from where Lee and I had once lived. As I bent to offer the tray to a guest, I heard someone behind me whisper,

"My God, doesn't that maid look an awful lot like Betty Marvin?" I hid my face and raced out of the room.

There were days I felt I couldn't keep up the constant travel in search of food and shelter. After having had the fortune, years ago, of an enormous home—an oasis—for me and my family, I couldn't believe I was down to this. I longed to have even a room to go back to every night, much less an entire house.

I'd call friends, trying not to make too much of my situation, but also to get messages left for me; it was the only way people could stay in touch. Finally, I caught an extremely lucky break, and once again it came from my old friend Robert Walker. He had left word to call him, and when I did, he told me he'd lost his caretaker at his second home in Cambria. Did I want the job? "The place needs a lot of maintenance, Betty," he told me, "but it's pretty up there." I felt a rush of relief. Robert and I made arrangements, and I drove up to Cambria, thanking whatever stars had been looking out for me.

The house was in a beautiful spot but indeed in need of work. The windows were covered in grime. I wondered if indeed there ever had been, as Robert put it, a "caretaker." No matter, the house would have one now.

It felt strange working at a place where I had spent many fun weekends playing. The acre of terraced garden had no automatic watering system and needed a lot of maintenance because the property was up for sale. This meant hauling miles of hose up and down hills. The three-story house with many windows was situated on a dirt road up on a hill; and every time a car would drive by, the windows I'd washed would get once again covered with dust. It was hard work, but my physical exhaustion was the perfect prescription for a good night's sleep.

My old Chrysler, after miles of going from job to job, was showing signs of its age. The thought of being stuck up in the country without a car seemed like the last straw.

Driving home on the freeway one evening after catering a birthday party near San Luis Obispo, I saw a patrol car pass me going in the opposite direction. The next thing I knew the car was behind me, red lights blinking, summoning me to pull over. *Oh, God, what now?* Cops scared me.

"Stay calm," I told Sadie as the patrolman approached.

"What's the problem, Officer?" I said.

"You're driving with your brights on. Show me your driver's license and step out of the car."

Now I was really scared. I'd had a couple of glasses of wine while cleaning up after the party. *What's the limit? No matter, I'm not drunk, just exhausted. It's only nine o'clock.* The next thing I knew I was walking a line and touching my nose. The cop's partner was checking my car for drugs. *Can he do that? I don't even know my rights. I hope Sadie doesn't attack him. In a way I wish she would.*

"You have to take a Breatholizer test," the cop said.

"But I walked the line and touched my nose."

"This is standard procedure."

"But I'm not drunk." Lee had told me I should never take a Breatholizer test if I'd been drinking. Funny I should remember that all of a sudden. In fact, Lee was stopped numerous times while driving drunk, but he was never asked to take any test whatsoever—just given a friendly warning to drive carefully and usually asked for an autograph. Amazing how people with money and power get away with it. I was obviously in a different class, where there was no bending of the rules. When I refused the test, I was put into the backseat of the patrol car and hauled off to jail.

I began to cry. "What about my dog?"

"She'll go to the shelter. Come on, honey," the cop said. "Be a big girl."

"I'm not your honey," I flashed back, infuriated by his rudeness. I told myself to be quiet, then ignored my own advice. "I'm a respectable woman and I'm not drunk."

"Save your breath, ma'am, it's all been said before. Here we go, out of the car." He opened the back door. We had arrived at the jail. After being humiliated with a mug shot and fingerprints, I was put into a cell while they figured out what to do with me. I lay down on the wooden bench, covered my body with the thin blanket, and prayed for a miracle. For my refusal to take the Breatholizer test I was charged with a DUI. I was to spend the night in jail.

But two hours later, thoroughly shaken, I was released. At the car pound I wrote a bad check on a closed account and drove home at dawn, worried about finding Sadie. I lay awake until my attorney's office opened, then called for help. The office loaned me money to cover my fines and get Sadie out of the pound. The DUI, however, stuck. I was to spend the next three months creeping once a week in my ailing Chrysler to traffic school. Except for one other student—an unfortunate, dignified elderly woman who had been pulled over while driving home after a couple of glasses of champagne at her son's wedding—I stuck out like a sore thumb among hardened alcoholics who were taking the course for the third or fourth time. The instructor warned me, like the others, that once I was in the system, I'd most likely be back. *Never*, I thought.

The rest of the time I was isolated in the pines surrounding Robert's house. The quiet, repetitive action of picking up pine needles from the dusty earth as the wind blew and hushed around me eventually drew me into a meditative state, and little by little I began to climb out of the pit. I began to write, and every day the words came more easily. I returned to making art, this time from objects I found around Robert's home and the surrounding grounds.

During the three years I spent with no roof of my own over my head, the building was lost in forclosure and I never knew whether I would recover financially or lose to a team of clever insurance lawyers defending the real estate brokers, real estate attorneys and accountant who had put me into this deal. Their lawyers were out to hold onto every last penny. The unscrupulous seller of the building, after declaring backruptcy, was still out of the state. Even if I won in court, I knew I could be facing appeal after appeal. In the end, my attorneys put it on the table: I was broke and would have to make a deal. They were caring, supportive, and smart, settling on the courtroom steps, as they say, making the best deal possible.

My long period of hanging on by my teeth was over. Not that I was financially whole again; I wasn't back where I had started before selling the building in Venice. But by now I was philosophical about the experience. Initially, I hadn't envisioned settling the lawsuit, knowing that what had happened to me was unjust. However, in that time I learned an invaluable lesson. With the loss of all the "stuff" of my life came a freedom I would never have known otherwise. Living day by day, fending for myself, and taking on the world alone—without Lee, without another man, without the cushion of capital and belongings—put me in touch with the importance of those things money can't buy.

Because of that experience, the growing homeless population in California began to dominate my thoughts. I spent the next several months creating "cardboard condos"—interpretations of the homeless shelters that filled southeast Los Angeles—and finally put them on exhibition in 1993.

But I was still hungry to document the homeless of different cultures, so with that in mind, I charted a one-year journey around the world, traveling solo with one piece of carry-on luggage. I photographed and interviewed the homeless in their natural habitats. It was fascinating finding homeless people in Tokyo, hidden away in the subway tunnels behind bonsai hedges. Their shoes were kept outside their cardboard condos and tiny shrines with Buddhas were inside. In spite of poverty, neatness was still their order of the day. I discovered in Indonesia the concept of homelessness did not exist. The home one is born into is "home" until death.

Right on, I thought. *Everyone should have a home.*

32

Playing House with Jolly Robert

After a year of exploration, I was unwinding in a rented flat in London. The phone rang. It was Robert Walker calling from Santa Barbara, California.

"Ready to come home, Betty?"

We laughed. This was Robert's usual opening line. But this time he wasn't kidding.

"I'm staying in a friend's place in Montecito. I don't think she's coming back. She's put her house on the market, and I can live here until it's sold."

"What about your other three houses?" I asked him. Robert had always lived grandly.

"Gone with the wind, honey. I'm quite at home here. Very close to the beach. Come live with me," he said rather suddenly. "You know we'd make excellent roommates. You cook, and I eat."

I said I'd think about it. We went on to other things. But he'd hit a nerve. I was tired of being away from home, and reality had caught up with me. I either had to go back to the United States and deal with the IRS, or keep traveling and never go back. I had been notified by my CPA that the IRS was treating the foreclosure on the building I had bought and lost in foreclosure as a sale, declaring it a capital gain. I had to prove that it was indeed a capital loss. I called Robert the next day.

"Oh, I'm so glad," he said when I told him I'd be coming. "You'll have your own suite and the rent's cheap. You'll love it. Lots of room."

There was lots of room, but almost all of it was crammed with Robert's enormous antique collection. He had emptied all of three houses into the one house we now shared at 100 Butterfly Lane in Montecito, the posh neighborhood of Santa Barbara. Rugs lay on top of rugs, and every inch of wall space was taken up by so much furniture that I had to walk sideways from one room to another. Thank God everything I owned was in storage. I'd brought nothing but my one bag of clothes from my trip around the world. I moved into the front bedroom overlooking the front garden, which Robert had filled with lovely pieces, including a sleigh bed, a chaise lounge, and an antique desk.

It was wonderful to be with Robert, who had put on a lot of weight since our last meeting but was still his jolly self. We sat over dinner catching up.

"Betty, I'm in trouble. I'm about to lose the agency."

"What are you talking about?"

"The other agents in my company wanted to buy me out," Robert confessed. "They threatened to take the clients, including my star actors, and leave if I didn't sell. I told them it was my company and it was not for sale."

"So?"

"So, I am still the proud owner of the famous Beverly Hills Century Artists Ltd.—with no artists. Now I can't get into my own office."

"What?"

"The IRS has put a padlock on the door. Is there more chicken?"

"You ate it all. Robert, what are you going to do?"

"Well, I really don't know," he said, suddenly turning toward the kitchen. "But let's not ruin a beautiful dinner. What's for dessert?"

Robert's world might have been collapsing, but for the most part he soldiered on, ignoring looming bankruptcy. He was always up with the sun, bright, cheerful, and enjoying his paper and coffee. It was fun to be living with my old friend after so much time, but I was concerned when he said he was in trouble.

"Honey, we need to get serious here. Look at these bills!" I said to Robert one day.

There was a stack of envelopes from collection agencies and lawyers on the sixteenth-century marble credenza in the foyer.

"Don't worry about it, Sweetie. Just throw 'em in a box. God! What a beautiful day! Let's go down to Tutti's for lunch."

"We can't afford to go out to lunch!"

"Oh, don't be such a killjoy. I've got to circulate, drum up some clients. C'mon, let's walk."

Once at Tutti's, Robert took a look through the window and instantly turned around, grabbing my arm. "Better keep going," he whispered into my ear, laughing. "Tutti's in there. He's blocked my credit. Thought he wouldn't be in till dinner. How about the Montecito Inn?"

"Is your credit any better there?" I asked wryly.

"I'll let you treat me this one time."

Celebrating Christmas 1994 with friends Martine and Robert

Walking back to our house, we saw people in the driveway. Two men with a tow truck were about to drive off with Robert's red Lexus coupe.

"Wait a minute, guys!" Robert yelled, trotting slowly up to the car. "I've got to get some stuff out of there."

They lowered the car back to the ground. "Make it snappy."

"Sure, sure. Betty, could you run in and get me a trash bag?" I sprinted into the house, grabbed a bag, and hurried out.

Robert had opened the trunk of the car. I stopped in my tracks. It was crammed with mail, all of it unopened bills from his office.

A few minutes later Robert's precious Lexus was towed away, and we were left there holding the bag.

"Be a darling and fix one of your fabulous gourmet meals this evening. Tab Hunter's coming to dinner. I've just signed him."

Robert was still wheeling and dealing, trying to conceal his financial crash from the industry. I'd never met Tab, the drop-dead gorgeous, top box office star at Warner Brothers in the fifties. I was happy to discover that, though he remained very handsome, he was not at all arrogant – a rare, wonderful quality for a successful actor. He was with his young partner, Allan, a producer. They had been together twenty-two years, longer than most Hollywood marriages last.

I served rack of lamb, Robert's favorite. The wine flowed as, between bites, Robert carried on about possible projects for Tab. But as soon as he finished his second serving of crème brûlée, he padded over to his favorite chair and, in moments, was snoring in front of the fire.

Tab, Allan, and I started to laugh.

"Let me get that for you," Tab said as I was toting the meat platter to the sink.

The three of us rolled up our sleeves and got to work cleaning up. Every few moments a loud snore would vibrate through the kitchen, and the three of us were lost in a fit of giggles. Finally, Robert settled into a snuffling sleep, and Tab, Allan, and I sat around the dining table.

Tab turned to me with his engaging smile. "Robert tells me you were living in Rome in 1969. I was there at the same time."

"Funny, Robert mentioned to me you were at Warner Brothers in the 1950s when my ex-husband was shooting there."

"Robert loves to talk," Tab smiled.

"It's odd we've never met before."

"Better late than never," he said, his blue eyes sparkling.

We stayed up all hours talking, a friendship forming as Robert slumbered on. Tab and I were attracted to each other even though we were very different – he being a gay, Catholic, Republican and I, a straight, nonreligious liberal. Perhaps it was because we were only three years apart in age and both Cancers, although he scoffed at taking seriously any of that "woo woo" science, as he called it. Tab teased me for being passionate about causes, yet I was to learn that he was always sweet, kind, and generous to everyone he met. Before long Tab, Allan and I became very close and spent much time together.

Tab, myself and Allan in Venice, Italy 1999

"Jesus, Robert, what on earth!" I exclaimed. He'd pulled up into the driveway in a clunker of a car. The fender was deeply dented from a recent wreck, and a piece of cardboard had replaced the right rear window. Pieces of the car threatened to fall off at any moment.

"Wheels, Betty! I have to have wheels! Obviously, this is just temporary. Anyway, come look at what I've found." He opened the back door and beckoned me over. "Give me a hand. You will not believe the work on this mirror—Italian Baroque, absolutely gorgeous."

I helped him inch the mirror slowly out of the car. It weighed a ton.

"Robert, where did you get this?"

"Estate sale. They were practically giving it away! We'll come back for the rest after we get this inside."

Looking back at the car, I saw it was loaded down with more antiques—lamps, candlesticks, and God knows what. I couldn't believe my eyes. When we got it all inside, I sat him down.

"Robert, this is crazy."

"What is crazy?"

"This," I said, motioning around me. "All this stuff. You keep buying when you should be selling! You need money. Stop going to estate sales and have one of your own. Have ten!"

Robert just laughed.

"I'm not kidding. I want to help you, but you've got to cooperate. I'll take out an ad in the paper and run the sale myself. Are you up for it?"

"Okay, okay. Anything to stop your carrying on. I'm starving. What's for dinner?"

I took out an ad in the local paper and spent two days organizing and pricing the pieces for sale. By 7:00 AM the following Saturday, we had a line snaking around the block.

"I told you people would come," I said to him excitedly.

"I'm not selling anything."

"Robert, come on. We're going to make some real money here."

"All right, let me finish my coffee and we'll open up the doors."

I picked up a bar stool that I knew would sell quickly, planning to place it up near the front. Putting it down, I saw the price on the leatherette seat. Robert had penned a *2* in front of my "*50.00.*

"Two hundred and fifty! Robert, no one is going to pay two hundred and fifty dollars for this thing!"

"Good. I don't want to sell it anyway."

"Robert, you can't have a sale unless you sell things."

In a panic, I started checking all of the price tags. Every single item had been marked up. As the sale started, I was still running around with a pen crossing off Robert's ridiculous prices. People would come up to me in confusion, point out a piece, and whisper, "Is that really a thousand dollars?"

"A hundred. Sorry, some of the tags were mixed up."

Deals closed quickly. Robert was oblivious, locked in conversation with an antiques dealer he knew. I suspected the guy would buy back a number of things Robert had bought from him—at a fraction of the price.

At the end of the day, the house finally quiet, I sat in the kitchen and counted the cash. In spite of Robert's attempted sabotage, I'd made $13,000. *Thought it was a little more,* I mused to myself as I went to find Robert and give him the tally. He was nowhere to be found.

Dinner was in the oven and I was sipping a glass of wine when I heard the front door open.

"Ow! Betty, I think I'm stuck."

I went to the door. Robert was trying to edge his bulky body and what appeared to be a child's piano into the house at the same time.

"Take a step backward and turn it the other way. What on earth is this?"

"Wait! You'll see!"

Finally in the living room, we set his new purchase down. It was an antique miniature, gold-leafed spinet piano, so small one had to get down on the floor to play it.

"For you," Robert wheezed, still getting his breath. "It's a thank-you gift."

"Robert, what am I going to do with this?"

He was on his knees playing a tune. "I thought we could play duets. Isn't it adorable?"

I was right about having made more at the sale than $13,000. We'd made $15,000—$13,000 in cash and $2,000 in a spinet piano. Robert looked around at the living room. Not only had we made some money, but we were down to three armchairs where once there had been nine.

"It's really quite a big house, isn't it?" Robert said very pleased, as if we'd just moved in. "Let's rearrange the furniture."

33

Settling In: Taking Inventory

Robert and I stayed together in Montecito for two years until the house was sold. It was time to move on. Robert rented an apartment in Santa Barbara, but I had trouble finding a rental that would accept dogs.

I wasn't convinced I would stay in Montecito. I'd made friends there, but the charm of that village had worn thin. It was too conservative, too proper, too "white bread and mayonnaise." I hardly ever saw anyone who was not a well-to-do Caucasian, and I missed diversity, being accustomed to the rich array of odd characters in my old digs of Venice and travels throughout the world. I extended my housing search, not sure I would like living anywhere in Santa Barbara. But I had grown to appreciate the beauty, ease, and comfort of this town. I could drive down the coast to Los Angeles for a day or two and get all the stimulation I needed. It was a good base from which to travel. I began exploring the hills and foothills on the Santa Barbara Westside, the only area I could afford. Friends were concerned about the threat of Latino gangs in that area, but after living in Venice, I wasn't so easily put off.

Following an "open house" sign led me to a beautifully restored 1905 Craftsman residence, with ten-foot ceilings, double-hung, leaded windows, and beautiful detailing throughout.

I called Tab. "I think I've found the house. Come give me a second opinion?"

He drove right over. I could see as he got out of his car the neighborhood didn't impress him. No two small houses lining the street were alike, and some were in disrepair. Tab was used to the well-tended estates of Montecito. He'd driven off the beaten track and didn't look too pleased.

"Sweet house," he murmured to me, looking around inside, "but you know what they say—location, location, location."

Still, by the time I'd walked through the house a second time, I knew I wanted it. There was something resonant of my childhood home, both inside and out. I fell for the green schoolyard across the street and the sight of people walking down the sidewalks. It would be good to be part of a real neighborhood again.

My 1905 Craftsman residence

The deal was done quickly. Before I knew it, I was buying a swing like the one on the old front porch of my grandparents' home.

I existed on three or four hours' sleep a night the first week there, unpacking boxes containing treasures I hadn't seen for seven years or more. Putting my Grandma's Haviland china into the cabinets in the dining room was deeply satisfying. The antique furniture I had saved from the home I had shared with Lee complemented the dark paneling of each room. The ecru silk quilt embroidered with colorful birds by Grandma Ebeling in 1900 was hung on the wall at the head of my bed.

Perhaps best of all was having a studio again. The two-car, detached garage lent itself easily to a space for making art. With canvasses, brushes, and paints in place, I moved on next to the garden, planting all the flowers I remembered from my childhood. A rose garden and my favorite trees—birch and jacaranda—were already there.

After roaming around for years, it was good to feel the ground beneath my feet. I knew I'd come home.

One Sunday morning I called Robert Walker to discuss his coming over for our regular Sunday evening dinner. There was no answer. *That's strange,* I thought. He always spent Sunday morning in bed, reading the paper and talking on the phone. I was ready to drive over and check things out when I had a phone call from Robert's brother, Jim.

"I'm sorry to tell you, Betty, but Robert died this morning. Heart attack."

I was shocked. Grief-stricken, I hung up and had a long cry over the loss of my dear friend of more than fifty years.

I joined "Project Food Chain," an organization of local chefs who met every Wednesday to prepare gourmet meals for those in need in the community, primarily terminally ill AIDS patients. A few months later we chartered a bus to Chinatown in Los Angeles to feast on dim sum. I found myself seated next to Julia Child, and we began chatting about this and that. A mutual friend passed by.

"I'm happy to see you two are getting acquainted. Julia, you know Betty was married to Lee Marvin."

"Who?" Julia said.

"You know, the movie star?"

"Sorry," Julia said. "I never heard of him." She turned to me. "I hope you aren't offended. I'm in the food business."

"Not at all," I said smiling, relieved that she had no idea who Lee was. In meeting Julia, my identity was my own.

We shared our love for Paris, including our favorite bistros and cafes, and began having regular dates for lunch, movies, and dinner out. Dining with Julia was fun, not in the least formal. She always went to the kitchen to give her compliments to the chef but was entirely candid in her private comments to me afterward. She never liked a restaurant that was too contrived, "studied" as she called it. She knew good food and hated pretense of any kind.

The first time I invited Julia to dinner was intimidating. Cooking for Julia Child was a bit like singing for Frank Sinatra: one felt no hope of measuring up. As I shopped, I reminded myself how down-to-earth she was and how effortlessly our friendship had formed. That evening she found me in the kitchen stirring risotto to accompany osso buco.

"What are you doing in here? Need any help?" Imagine: Julia Child, my sous-chef. She checked the risotto. "Not necessary to keep stirring once you've put in the first cup of boiling chicken broth. Just pour in the rest, stir it through, put on the lid, and come have a glass of wine."

"Delicious," she announced at the end of the meal. "Betty, you're a good cook."

The relief in my smile must have been palpable.

Celebrating Julia Child's ninetieth birthday in 2003

Julia's health began to deteriorate and she spent more and more time in the hospital, first with an infection from a knee replacement, then increasing kidney problems She went from being a spry, active woman to becoming an invalid in a wheelchair. I understood, but selfishly I was sad when Julia chose to give up having constant medical treatment and let nature take its course. She died in August 2004, two days before her ninety-second birthday. I knew how much I would miss her, but she had led a fabulous life and I was grateful to be a part of it. Every holiday I feel her presence at my annual Gourmet Christmas Cook-off, her favorite party. I still laugh at the memory of her accidentally sitting on the Yuletide log while resting on the edge of the kitchen table.

Funny, the things that come to people who create art, often out of the blue or dug up from some long-ago passing thought. I don't remember why I started thinking about the old mink coat Lee had given me. That coat had been everywhere, playing many roles, acting as my lifesaver in the Paris fire. I found it in the back of a closet, hauled it into the studio, grabbed my art shears, and began cutting the lining, tearing the pelts into pieces of fur. I felt as free as when I was throwing paint. The mink was going to make one last stand.

I began making a series of pine boxes, satin-lined and covered entirely in mink. Each box was filled with individual objects of desire: mock wedding rings, love letters, dried roses, and lyrics to torch songs. I call the collection *What I Did for Love*. The pieces have been shown in several California and international exhibits.

My kids, all unmarried now, have grown into beautiful, bright adults who are striving to make a living in the arts. Christopher is an accomplished drummer and artist, at present creating mosaics from sea glass he collects at the beach. He lives in Santa Barbara. Courtenay is also an artist. She lives in Ventura and has returned to college to become an architect. Cynthia is a freelance costume designer in television and has a sterling reputation as a gifted quilt maker. Claudia and her longtime partner, Tim, have their own construction company in Golden, Colorado. Qualities in my children such as humor, talent, and good character I found so dear fifty years ago bind us together now.

Courtenay, Christopher, and Cynthia, 2007

My twenty-seven-year-old grandson, Matthew, Cynthia's son, met Ting online. She called herself Tim and he thought he was corresponding with a Chinese boy. After discovering the truth, he traveled several times to China to be with her, then brought her home with him and they were married. After watching what his grandma, mom, uncle, and aunts have gone through to make it as creative artists, Matthew chose another route. He graduated as an economics major from my alma mater, UCLA. Finally, someone in the family has a steady job.

Ting and Matthew's wedding 2006

My artist friend Norton and I bought a stretch of land overlooking the sea in lower Baja, Mexico. There I designed and constructed an earth structure with sandbags, barbed wire, and adobe—a home without timber, steel, or concrete that cost almost nothing to build. When I spend time in Baja I live in "Castillo de Arena," a sand castle that is water—and fireproof and stays cool in the summer and warm in the winter.

"Castillo de Arena," my winter retreat in Baja, Mexico

Last year I celebrated my eightieth birthday with family and friends. I even received the annual card from my college boyfriend, Bob Horton. I toasted them all and the dear hearts who have left this life but are with me in spirit. I am grateful for the many adventures that have brought me this far in what seems like a short time.

Life is good.

ABOUT THE AUTHOR

Betty Marvin lives in Santa Barbara, California, and spends time during the winter in her sand castle on the coast of Baja, Mexico. At eighty-one, she is busy designing environmental structures, making conceptual art, painting, and writing.

Betty Marvin gains independence within a Hollywood life, first as Joan Crawford's nanny, then Lee Marvin's wife, and finally becoming a free-spirited artist.

Made in the USA
Las Vegas, NV
15 March 2022

45622492R00142